Summit's Glory

Summit's Glory

Sketches of Buchtel College and
The University of Akron

George W. Knepper

Drawings by Bruce R. Armstrong

The University of Akron Press

Dr. Phillip R. Shriver, then President Emeritus of Miami University and a practicing historian, delivered an eloquent address at the 1988 Founder's Day in which he urged this university to celebrate its history and tradition; he suggested a book of this sort as one way of doing it. During that same period, the newly established University of Akron Press decided that a University-centered book would be an appropriate way to initiate publication. These dreams became reality through the generosity and concern of Paul E. Martin, Class of '35. It is a gesture worthy of John R. Buchtel!

Daniel Nelson, professor of history and director of The University of Akron Press, has guided the work from its inception. He read the manuscript and greatly improved it with his suggestions. John Miller, University Archivist, also gave the work a careful reading. Caroline Pardee, Class of '32, assisted with the appendix. I thank each of them and assume full responsibility for sins of commission; sins of omission, on the other hand, are inevitable in a work of this selectivity and brevity. I am especially grateful for the illustrations by Bruce Armstrong, professor of art, who has handled skillfully the problem of finding ways to illustrate complex themes. Mia Hahn O'Connor typed the manuscript and saw it through many revisions. Her work, always accomplished in good spirit, is much appreciated.

GEORGE W. KNEPPER
Akron, Ohio, March 1990

Summit's Glory

"O'er Old Buchtel, Summit's Glory, waves the gold and blue"
Alma Mater by Augustus B. Church

education in the liberal Christian tradition. Others had been lured by the special rates the railroads offered for the occasion, thanks to which "hundreds of people who would not otherwise have done so, came for the sake of the ride." By eleven o'clock, when the last train disgorged its passengers, there were at least 5,000 strangers in Akron who had to find their way along streets already thronged with thousands of local citizens. It was a festive throng despite the rain. Band music and frequent salutes were constant reminders that this was a special day. Indeed, the Excelsior Gun Squad had welcomed the Glorious Fourth at midnight with a rousing twenty-gun salute; the Buckeye Gun Squad, by contrast, "showed their good sense by waiting until sunrise when their cannon thundered forth 37 times."

The local dignitaries, having taken stock of the weather, decided to postpone the ceremonies until two o'clock. As this decision was announced, the skies cleared and the sun came out, drying the land and relieving the frustration that had been building in the crowd. The visitors were further cheered by lunch. The basket dinner planned for Grace Park had been washed out, but a cooperative crowd was shepherded into the Phoenix, Empire, and Temperance halls, where "an abundance of provisions" were spread on hastily erected tables. Hundreds of visitors were accommodated at the Empire House while the Knights Templar, Marble's Band, and the 29th Ohio Volunteer Infantry held a grand banquet in Commerce Hall.

By two o'clock the procession had formed on Howard Street. There were 22 units in the parade, among them several bands, the Grand Army of the Republic (Civil War veterans), the Masons, the Odd Fellows, the Knights of Pythias, the Father Matthew Temperance Society, clergy, city officials, and "citizens." Turning east on Market Street, the parade moved up the hill to Elm Street (now College Street), where it turned right and proceeded to the College grounds with bands playing and banners flying. Not even an interruption "caused by two drunken men in a buggy breaking into the ranks near the railway bridge and scattering people right and left" spoiled the spirit of the marchers, although it may have troubled members of the Father Matthew Temperance Society. Many banners, decorations, and mottoes hung along the line of march. One, which attracted considerable attention, read:

> Greeley for President, Buchtel for College,
> Akron for Enterprise, Beauty and Knowledge.

A great throng awaited the procession on the College grounds. The cornerstone was to be laid according to traditional Masonic ritual, and as soon as the procession reached the appointed spot, the Masons gathered in their proper places. The Reverend Everett L. Rexford of Columbus, one of the prime movers in the founding of the school, then delivered a prayer. Earnest as he was, the good reverend probably would have prayed even more fervently for the College's well-being had he foreseen that within seven years he would be its president.

The officers of the Grand Lodge of Ohio then proceeded with the ceremonies. The three-foot-square cornerstone bore the inscription

> Centenary of Universalism
> in
> America
> 1870
> This Stone Laid July 4th, 1871
> By A. H. Newcomb, G. M., F. & A. M.
> A. L. 5871

A cavity in the stone contained a casket filled with church publications, the *Akron Daily Beacon* and other newspapers, a copy of the Bible, a list of officers of the College and of the participating Masons, and samples of American coins. With the singing of "The Origin of Buchtel College," written by W. Milton Clarke of Akron, the placement of the stone was complete. The crowd eased forward in anticipation as the speaker, a plain, grandfatherly man, rose on the platform.

Horace Greeley, editor of the *New York Tribune* and a prominent Universalist, had been the center of attention since his arrival the evening before, when he had been greeted at the depot with "a spontaneous ovation by thousands who gathered . . . to catch a glimpse of the great philosopher." Well known to Akron's citizens through his columns, which local newspapers often reprinted, he had been a critic of Lincoln's conduct of the Civil War and was now a critic of the Republican administration of President U. S. Grant. He was soon to challenge that administration by becoming a candidate for the presidency. Tradition has it that Akron was first in expressing support for these ambitions because of the "Greeley for President" banner that hung along the parade route and because of the lyrics of Clarke's song:

> And when a full report is made
>   Of this great celebration,
> Remember that the Tribune's head
>   May head this glorious nation.
> But if this thing should fail to be,
>   It sure would be a pity,
> For the White House is his proper place
>   And not in New York City.

While the young Mr. Rexford shielded him from the hot sun with an umbrella, Greeley launched into his topic, "Human Conceptions of God as They Affect the Moral Education of Our Race." In a strong voice that belied his 60 years, Greeley developed the thought that "a vivid conception of God's active presence, and conscious, intelligent interest in human affairs, is indispensable" to the moral education and development of the human race. In the education of the intellect man had made great strides, but there remained those who blend "the knowledge of a Humboldt with the ethics of a Dick Turpin" (a celebrated English robber), and their number "seems to be increasing." To offset this trend, education should be grounded in religion:

This, then, I apprehend, is the proper work of the College: to appreciate, and measure . . . the gigantic strides which Physical Science is making in our day, yet be not swept away by them; . . . to welcome all that is true and beneficent in the impetuous currents of modern thought, but not exaggerate their breadth and depth; to proffer a genial and gracious hospitality to whatever is nobly new, yet hold fast, and from time to time assert . . . that simple affirmation of the untaught Judean peasant who long ago perceived and proclaimed that GOD IS LOVE!

On a more practical note Greeley offered "a few words in reference to the education inculcated by our Colleges at large. It is too superficial for the age." Although there had been a great advance in every department of human endeavor, "there has not been a corresponding stride in the curriculum of college studies." He hoped to see the day when Buchtel College would "graduate a great and glorious body of young and earnest men in engineering, sci-

ence, and a hundred different pursuits, where knowledge is of great benefit to human kind."

The speech was well received by the crowd, which then called repeatedly for John R. Buchtel, whose generosity had made the College possible. He responded in "one of his off-hand unreportable speeches," with great feeling thanking those who had participated in the day's events and pledging that the College would bring honor and pride to Akron and the state. It would be "first class" in every respect. He reassured the orthodox among the crowd who looked askance at the Universalist brand of Christianity: "We don't intend to pull a shingle from a single church, but will unite in suppressing evil and building up the morals and character of the city." These remarks were greeted with "thunderous applause." The ceremony was now complete; the parade re-formed and made its way back to Howard Street.

Like the bright, balmy weather that succeeded the morning's rain, the enthusiasm and concern of the crowd was a propitious sign of the support the College would receive in days to come. Many of those gathered on the College grounds lingered after the ceremony. A large number of them made their way the short distance to Buchtel's house, where a steady stream of visitors crowded around to shake Greeley's hand. Rexford remembered the scene 50 years later:

Mr. Greeley sat in a large easy chair under one of the great evergreens at the northeast section of the lawn. It was an inspiring scene when the old farmers of Summit County and surrounding counties came by the hundreds to shake his hand, while many said, "Mr. Greeley, you educated me politically through the columns of the Tri-bune"—they divided the name of the paper in this way—and Mr. Greeley would bow and smile in his fatherly way, and sometimes would say, "Well, well, I hope I did not lead you wrong," or words similar.

At 8:30, Babcock's Band came by to serenade the crowd. Toasts were proclaimed from the front steps of Buchtel's residence. In response to a toast to Universalism, Greeley criticized the evangelical churches for excluding Universalists from the main body of Christianity: "We of the Universalist faith are out of the great body of Christian churches at the present time, not because we deserve to be, but because they say we are not orthodox. Our case is similar to that of members of colored churches. Being denied admission to churches of their white brethren, they build for themselves." After explaining and lauding Universalist views, Greeley appealed for hope and trust.

More toasts, more responses, more band music. Buchtel, called again by the crowd, expanded on his earlier statements to reassure those who were not comfortable about the Universalist persuasion. When the matter of a college was first broached to him in a letter from the Reverend George Messenger of Springfield, said Buchtel, he had written in reply that he would give $25,000 toward locating such an institution in Akron, but he would have done the same for any college, under whatever auspices. He was proud to think that the institution would not graduate Methodists, or Baptists, or Universalists, but men, and women too, for he wanted them to be on equal terms with the men. This brought loud cheers.

The day's festivities closed on this felicitous note. The special trains had departed long ago, and now the throng at the Buchtel residence dispersed. The next day work continued on the great College building, which would take more than a year to complete.

2

Ohio Universalists
Build a College

The laying of the cornerstone for the College building occurred just four years after the Ohio Universalist Convention decided to build a school in Ohio. The Universalists arrived at this decision somewhat late, since nearly every Christian denomination had built at least one college in the state prior to 1871. Several denominationally inspired or controlled colleges were within a few hours' journey from Akron: Wooster was run by Presbyterians, Hiram by Disciples of Christ; Mount Union College and Baldwin University (later Baldwin-Wallace) were founded under Methodist auspices. And although Western Reserve and Oberlin had no direct denominational connections, the former had a Presbyterian tie and the latter was indebted to Congregationalists. Methodists, Presbyterians, and others had taken pains to see that their children received an education in surroundings that were theologically and morally safe, and Universalists might well follow their lead.

Universalists were not as sensitive to theological partic-

year the Ohio Convention reaffirmed its intention of establishing a denominational school "whenever a suitable location may be secured and requisite funds pledged" and hired the Reverend Henry Miller of Dublin, Indiana, to seek the necessary pledges. Miller was also to work with the Committee on Education to select a location for the new school.

It proved easier to raise $50,000 than it did to select a site. Several towns—Oxford, Kent, and Mt. Gilead—made serious bids for the school. Oxford was eliminated because it already had a surfeit of colleges. Kent was rejected because periodic flare-ups of fever gave it a reputation as an "unhealthy place." This left Mt. Gilead as the prime contender, and it had much to offer. It was centrally located in the state; it was situated on high ground and was reported to be a healthy place; it had a strong Universalist congregation, and its businessmen quickly subscribed the necessary $10,000.

But Willson was not willing to concede the prize to Mt. Gilead. Disappointed that his own parish, Kent, had lost out, he set about trying to secure the school for Akron, just twelve miles from Kent. This thriving young manufacturing city of some 10,000 people boasted an impressive number of talented and successful entrepreneurs, many of them philanthropically inclined. Long before the Civil War, Akron had had a strong Universalist church whose congregation, unlike many in the denomination, included a number of powerful and influential members. Internal dissension had split the membership, however, and its property was sold, leaving the Akron Universalists without a church.

Among Akronites with Universalist sympathies was

John R. Buchtel, President of the Buckeye Mower and Reaper Company and a public-spirited citizen. He often attended the Kent church and was known to Willson. Late in 1869, Buchtel had been approached by persons interested in obtaining the school for Akron. Although he expressed sympathy for the project, he made it clear that he intended to give his money to the founding of a free public library in Akron. The matter thus appeared to be closed, but it was soon reopened by other developments.

The Universalists of Akron, though lacking a congregational organization, met frequently for services, and on Sunday, January 9, 1870, a visiting minister, the Reverend Henry L. Canfield, spoke to them at Empire Hall. The weather was bitterly cold, and Canfield was grateful for an invitation to share the hospitality of Mr. Avery Spicer, a lifelong adherent of the "liberal religion." That evening Spicer's two daughters, their husbands, and Sanford M. Burnham, the Summit County Auditor, stopped by for a visit. They were all interested in the Ohio Convention's effort to establish a school, and since Canfield was close to this work, he was in a position to inform them of the progress being made.

During the discussion the group became convinced that Akron was the proper location. They felt that the ideal site for the school would be on the grounds of the old Spicer Hill Cemetery, recently abandoned, which was located on high ground with a commanding view to the west. They also felt certain that John R. Buchtel was the proper person to provide the financial support. They talked themselves into a state of considerable enthusiasm about Akron's prospects. As Canfield described it, "we built a 'Castle in the air' and called it a Universalist Academy."

and eight were laymen. Of the latter, six were Akronites identified as "resident freeholders of Summit County."

The corporators then took the legal steps required to establish the college as a functioning unit. They differed on only one important item—the naming of the college. From the first some favored "Buchtel College," but others expressed the fear that this name would be corrupted by detractors into "Bucktail College." A compromise, "Buchtel Universalist College," pleased no one.

The resolution of this problem was described years later by Henry Canfield, who was present at the meeting as a corporator and trustee:

Finally, it was decided to ask Mr. Buchtel if he had any wish or choice in the matter of a name for the college. He was called in, and the question was put in plain words, "Mr. Buchtel, have you anything to suggest, or any wish to express, with regard to the name the college shall bear?" "Gentlemen," said he, "this is to be your college, not mine. I mean to help it financially as I may be able. If I live and am prospered I intend to give the college someday one hundred thousand dollars. You may call the college what you please." It was moved at once [by Henry Blandy] and voted unanimously that the institution be known as Buchtel College.

Canfield made it clear that Buchtel's intentions did not sway the decision:

If anyone reading these lines is moved to say or think that John R. Buchtel bought the name of the college for himself, let me say that such a person has no just conception of the spirit of the occasion. If we had felt that he had made a bid for the name, it would have been given reluctantly, if at all.

Buchtel, said Canfield, was a "great-hearted man" who, though he enjoyed the esteem and good opinion of others, was "not in the market to purchase applause."

The work of the corporators was approved enthusiastically by the Ohio General Convention held in June 1870 in Kent. Resolutions honoring the accomplishment passed unanimously. One of the resolutions gave a vote of confidence to the founders and to Buchtel by gratefully recognizing "the wisdom that gives the Institution his name."

3

John Richards Buchtel
Ohio College Builder

hen the Buchtel College Board of Trustees elected officers, it must have been evident to all that John R. Buchtel was a natural for the presidency of the Board. It is customary for colleges to eulogize their founders and chief contributors, but Buchtel could stand on his record. To the men who elected him as their leader, he was not just the principal contributor of funds; he was an experienced businessman who always made time to support his city's many activities. His philanthropy was well-known, although he made no show of it. His contributions to the little College named in his honor were vital to its very existence from its founding until his death in 1892.

Buchtel's story is in the rags-to-riches tradition that we like to think of as typically American. Born January 18, 1820, on a small farm in Green Township, then in Stark County but now in Summit County, he was of medium height, broad across the shoulders, physically powerful and tough, but of a peaceful disposition. In later years he wore a beard, the kind known as "chin whiskers." His full head of hair stayed with him to the end of his life. He was forceful and somewhat blunt in manner and speech, but his bluntness was tempered by a cheerful outlook. To an unusual degree he had the ability to get the job done, whatever it was, and to enlist others in his support. Early in life he demonstrated a kind of perseverance that would be called stubbornness had it been less constructive, and there were numerous times when every bit of that perseverance was required to keep the College alive.

In a society that still placed more value on what a man could do than on his formal educational credentials, John Buchtel was not unduly handicapped by his lack of formal education. It has been said that at age 21 he could scarcely write his own name. This may be an exaggeration, but the spelling and grammar in his few surviving letters are decidedly deficient. Like so many self-made men of his time, he seemed determined, despite his lack of learning, to see that others had a chance to obtain the schooling that he had missed.

As a young man, he was given 100 acres of farmland by his father on condition that he pay off a $700 encumbrance on the property. This he successfully did, and with his stake in life secured, he married Elizabeth Davidson, whose family had come to the Akron area from Pennsylvania some years earlier. The Buchtels had no children.

John then sold his farm in order to purchase 210 acres later known as the Thornton farm, a tract in the vicinity of modern Thornton Street. There, by using advanced agricultural techniques, he produced crops superior to those of his skeptical neighbors. Selling out at a profit, he next bought substantial acreage from Colonel Simon Perkins on what is now the near west side of Akron, and once again proved the skeptics wrong by farming and lumbering it profitably.

He was about to move again, this time to LaPorte County, Indiana, when he was offered a job as salesman for Ball, Aultman Company of Canton, manufacturers of the Ohio mower and reaper. Succeeding in that position, he helped persuade that company in 1864 to open an independent branch operation in Akron to manufacture the "Buckeye," an improved machine invented by Lewis Miller. He supervised construction of the plant and took charge as the new company's president. In large part through his influence, Akron became a center of the farm machinery industry, a position it was to hold until the 1890s, when the McCormick interests of Chicago absorbed what was left of the industry in Akron. Buchtel also helped to develop a number of related firms: an iron company, a rolling mill, a knife works, a twine factory, and a chain works. Concurrently he helped form a bank that was to be important in financing Akron's industrial growth.

Buchtel's most spectacular business venture was the purchase and development of 2,000 acres of mineral lands in southern Ohio for the Akron Iron Company, in which he had an interest. In 1876–77 he personally directed the development of coal and iron ore resources in the Hocking Valley and the erection there of what was at the time the largest blast furnace in Ohio. He also supervised the building of a company town to house the immigrant workers who had recently arrived from southern and eastern Europe, and he donated land for a Catholic church, an opera house, and a cemetery. It was an unusually well-ordered company town, and in recognition of his kindnesses the inhabitants named it in his honor. Though it has been transformed through the years, Buchtel, Ohio, is still on the map. In 1887, while working strenuously in the Hocking Valley, Buchtel suffered a stroke that paralyzed his lower body. He spent the last five years of his life in a wheelchair.

As he prospered in business, Buchtel spent an increasing amount of time serving in various public capacities. For many years he was a trustee of Portage Township, which at that time embraced most of Akron. He was a leading spirit in the Akron Library Association and helped to establish a free public library in 1877. He served many years as treasurer of the Summit County Agricultural Society. He was moderator of the newly re-formed Universalist congregation. And through it all he donated generously to virtually every church and worthy cause in Akron.

Buchtel joined the Republican party in its formative years. He was a strong supporter of the Union and the Lincoln administration, and during the Civil War he raised money tirelessly to pay bounties for volunteers, sparing Akron men who would otherwise have been drafted. He did not serve in the army, not even as a "hundred day" man in 1864, when many of his Akron business associates were rushing to the defense of Washington. Rather he paid a substitute, one W. S. St. John, a fifer, to serve in his stead.

After the war, Buchtel was a presidential elector, dutifully casting his ballot in 1872 for U. S. Grant. Two years later he abandoned the Republican party temporarily to run for the state office of Secretary of State on the Prohibitionist ticket. Some scoffers and doubters questioned his

4

Constructing a Campus

 college campus is a magnet for those attracted to academic life. Some campuses develop along orderly, predetermined lines, but Buchtel College, like Topsy, "just grew." Buchtel's first building was a brick house fronting on Middlebury Road (Buchtel Common), which the trustees purchased as a residence for the college presidents. This building, later called Phillips Hall, was torn down in 1946 to make way for Ayer Hall. When it was occupied by Sullivan McCollester in the 1870s, its spacious grounds included a barn and a garden, and a carriage path ran alongside the house.

Akron was chosen as the location of the new College in part because of the availability of an adequate campus site. The Spicer Hill Cemetery, a quarter mile southeast of John R. Buchtel's Buckeye Works, had been supplanted as a burying ground by the newly developed Akron Rural (Glendale) Cemetery. The Spicer Hill Cemetery deed was transferred to Buchtel College, the bodies buried there were removed to Akron Rural, and the burial grounds were prepared for the new College building.

One wonders how thoroughly the job of vacating graves

was performed. Frank Payne, Class of '84, recalled "the early years of the college, before the trees were planted and when every rainfall gouged out deep runnels in the clayey soil and disclosed full many a human bone." Nevertheless, at least 64 bodies were transferred to Akron Rural before ground was broken for the College building on March 15, 1871.

Meanwhile the trustees had requested various architects to submit plans for the proposed building. Those submitted by Thomas W. Silloway of Boston were selected, causing the *Boston Advertiser* to report that "eastern experience and talent" had been chosen. At a meeting in December 1870, Silloway explained his plans to the Trustees and led them on a tour of the College grounds, where they "determined the exact location of the proposed new building." Construction was entrusted to Noah Carter of Akron.

Work progressed rapidly. No records remain to tell us what the building cost, but the Trustees initially set aside $30,000 to $40,000 for this purpose. It was soon apparent that this would not be sufficient, principally because Silloway's plans called for a far more elaborate and extensive building than anyone had envisioned. However, it so captured the Trustees' enthusiasm that they resolved to seek additional funds. An estimated $160,000 to $200,000 was ultimately spent to complete the building and to furnish it.

By September 1872 the great building, at that time Akron's most impressive, was ready for use except for some interior finishing work. It loomed over the city and dominated it. This massive structure—240 feet long, 54 feet wide, and five stories high—was crowned by a blunt tower flanked on each side by narrow towers through which entrances led into the building. Identical wings ex-

was so heavy and so well imbedded that it tipped the crane whose powerful winches attempted to pull it from its moorings.

Another addition to the College grounds was an enormous ornamental cast-iron urn situated on the front lawn. It came from Buchtel's residence. The urn, planted annually, was a familiar sight until its removal in the 1960s, when it became apparent that its Victorian character contrasted unhappily with the more modern look of neighboring buildings.

An elaborate iron fence was erected around the campus in 1884. It was ornamental in part, but was also designed to prevent neighborhood boys from using the College grounds as a shortcut on their way to the Akron High School, just two blocks away.

The high point of campus improvement in the 1880s was the building of a gymnasium. As early as 1880, some of the students obtained plans from a local architect, Frank Weary, "for a cheap but attractive structure 44 by 66 feet with a bowling alley attached." The cost of this building was estimated at $800, but even this small sum was impossible to raise without support from the Board. The students' enthusiasm persisted, however, and in 1886–87 a considerable sum was pledged during a successful fundraising campaign directed by President Orello Cone.

The new structure was formally dedicated on February 22, 1888. It was named Crouse Gymnasium in honor of Akron businessman George W. Crouse, who had donated about half the required money. "The finest gym west of the Alleghenies" contained a playing floor, a bowling alley, a running gallery eleven feet above the gymnasium floor, a small visitor's gallery, and dressing, bathing, and

apparatus rooms. This fine facility encouraged the faculty
to require physical exercise of all students. With the completion of Buchtel Field in 1892 and a batting cage alongside the gym in 1893, Buchtel College had first-rate sports
facilities.

While Crouse Gym was building, Charles S. Howe, Professor of Mathematics, secured $3,700 to build and equip
a small observatory just east of the main College building.
But Howe left the faculty after six years, and the observatory fell into disuse. In any event, Akron's smoke-filled
skies were not conducive to stargazing.

The mood of happy expectation that grips a college just
before a holiday was much in evidence at Buchtel on December 20, 1899, the day before the fall term was to close.
The Delta Gammas were meeting in their room, and a
faculty meeting was in progress, when, shortly before five
o'clock, a man rushed into West Hall shouting that the
building was on fire. It was promptly evacuated, and two
fire companies arrived quickly with their horse-drawn,
steam-driven engines. Within five minutes of their arrival
a general alarm went out, bringing to campus Akron's
entire department. The blaze seems to have started under
the eaves at the east end of the building, but it spread
quickly into a general conflagration. Workmen on their
way home dropped their dinner pails and rushed to help
faculty, students, and policemen to remove whatever could
be salvaged from the building. Books, furniture, apparatus, whatever objects could be grabbed, were taken to
Crouse Gym. At the end of an hour several narrow escapes forced the police to suspend all further salvage efforts.

the president's role, were at that time exercised by the Board of Trustees. As long as John R. Buchtel lived and served as president of the Board, he personally directed much of this day-to-day activity with the assistance of the secretary of the Board, first A. B. Tinker and later Charles R. Olin.

There were strains in this system. During the last quarter of the nineteenth century college administration was becoming more bureaucratic, and specialization of function foretold the end of the casual paternalistic practices of the past. When Augustus B. Church became Buchtel's president in 1901, he assumed a much broader responsibility than his predecessors and the president's role emerged much as we know it today. This transition was effected by making President Church a Trustee of the College. His fellow Trustees soon elected him president of the Board. Following Church's untimely death in 1912, this consolidated presidency was assumed by young Parke Kolbe, who presided over the College's transition to municipal university status. Kolbe added yet another element to the president's role, the political leadership required of an institution that depended on public tax money.

Buchtel's nineteenth-century presidents had a number of characteristics in common. With the exception of Professor Charles M. Knight, who served as interim president for one year (1896–97), and Parke R. Kolbe, who held the reins in Buchtel's final months, they were all ordained Universalist clergymen; each taught moral philosophy; each preached regularly and took part in denominational affairs; and each was of small town background. But such superficial similarities are inconsequential. It is more interesting to note some individual characteristics.

Sullivan McCollester (1872–78), handsome, lean, with wavy hair and flowing mutton-chop whiskers, took a personal interest in his students. This New Hampshire native lived with his wife and son in the president's house (on the site of Ayer Hall), where he kept a garden and some hogs. The president had immediate access to his student charges. He taught them, preached at them, and even nursed them on occasion. Although he had the confidence of the Board, McCollester was the innocent victim of church quarrels in which student factions were enlisted, and his early resignation from office was prompted by student pressures. He returned to the ministry he had left, traveled widely and published accounts of his trips, and lived to a serene old age, maintaining the whole time a warmly supportive interest in Buchtel's growth.

His young successor, Everett Rexford (1878–80), pastor of the local Universalist congregation, had a strong face set off by pince-nez glasses and side-whiskers. A "stormy petrel," he preferred the pulpit to the presidency. After two productive years in office he resigned to assume a pastorate in Detroit, spurred on, no doubt, by the backlash from a bitter public feud that he carried on in the local newspaper with the rector of the Church of Our Savior, Episcopal. Like McCollester before him, he was still alert and concerned with the College's fate well beyond his ninetieth year.

Orello Cone (1880–96) was Buchtel's reluctant president. A compactly built man who, like his predecessors, sported side-whiskers, Cone was a distinguished scholar and professor of Biblical languages and literature at St. Lawrence University, the Universalist stronghold in Canton, New York. He was in no hurry to accept the initial call to become Buchtel College's third president. Assuming he wanted a more favorable arrangement, John R. Buchtel offered to let him stay at his own residence and use the horses and carriage free of charge. To everyone's apparent surprise, Cone refused the offer; but he had not reckoned with the tenacity of John Buchtel once that stubborn man's mind was set. It took a special meeting between the scholar and the blunt businessman, held in the Boston offices of a Universalist newspaper, before Cone was satisfied and accepted the call to Akron.

Though Cone was a Universalist clergyman, he found denominational expectations onerous. While corresponding with Mary Jewett concerning her possible appointment to the chair of English literature, he wrote that he was under strong pressure to appoint a Universalist. But, he said, "I shall not allow myself to be influenced by the *mere fact* of religious belief or association. I shall recommend the best qualified candidate regardless of theological opinions."

The pressure was great enough, however, that Cone wrote to Jewett a week later to say that if she accepted the appointment he would like her to attend the Universalist church as an example for the girls. "Could you give us a part of your heart, at least, in case you should find our preacher acceptable?" he asked somewhat wistfully. She could, and she did.

After sixteen years as president of Buchtel, Cone resigned, speeded on his way by disaffected students and alumni who deplored, among other things, his lack of enthusiasm for the football team. At the time of his departure the city was in the midst of a severe economic depression, and the College's finances were in disarray. Cone could ill afford to offend the athletic boosters.

The only layman to serve as president of the college in the nineteenth century was Professor Knight, the same man who later inaugurated the first collegiate courses in rubber chemistry. A vigorous-looking man whose luxuriant mustache flowed into side-whiskers, Knight served as president during the academic year 1896–97, when the college was in dire financial straits. He had all the qualities to make an outstanding president, but he was one of those rare persons who know their true vocation, and he preferred to return to his classroom and students at the first opportunity. It was said of Charles Knight that "he would have made an excellent president could he have won his own consent." On relinquishing the presidency, Knight was awarded an honorary Doctor of Science degree and was also appointed first Dean of the Faculty. Ironically, however, the letter informing him of these honors also stated that his salary was to be reduced ten percent.

Knight's successor, the fully bearded pastor of the local Universalist church, Ira Priest (1897–1901), rounded out the century. He was president at the time of the disastrous fire of 1899. During this unhappy period, Priest became the focus of student and alumni discontent, and, like McCollester and Cone before him, found it prudent to resign. He then entered business life in Akron.

Augustus B. Church (1901–1912), the last of Buchtel's Universalist clergyman presidents, was, as we have noted, a bridge to more modern administrative practices. Handsome, distinguished, and kindly disposed to students and staff, he was minister of the local Universalist congregation as well as College president. He presided over the removal of Buchtel College from Universalist sponsorship (1907), a move that transformed Buchtel into a nondenominational private liberal arts college. Bedeviled by one financial crisis after another, Church looked for expedients to salvage the College, including an unsuccessful effort to join forces with another failing Universalist school, Lombard College of Galesburg, Illinois. He died in November 1912 from pneumonia brought on by exhaustion and sitting through a football game in inclement weather. (President Cone would not have made that mistake!) With his passing the era of the old-time college president came to an end.

Buchtel College lived on for another thirteen months following Church's death. During this time its president was a "faculty brat," Parke R. Kolbe. The son of Professor Carl Kolbe, young Parke grew up on the Buchtel campus, often attending his father's classroom, where the four-year-old lad would "astound" the class with his precocious fluency in German. He earned a doctorate from Germany's Heidelberg University, married Lydia Voris, the daughter of a former Trustee, and succeeded his father as professor of modern languages. Seen by many as the perfect young leader to salvage Buchtel's fortunes, he did exactly that by organizing the transfer of its assets to the City of Akron and giving the private college new life as The Municipal University of Akron.

On the whole, Buchtel College fared well with her presidents. None was a knave or a fool. Each appears to have given his best in the face of formidable difficulties. They provided the base on which those who lead The University of Akron stand today.

6

Students of Old Buchtel

arpenters' chips and wood shavings still littered the floors of Old Buchtel when students appeared for classes in September 1872. For the first arrivals everything was new, not just the building. These students set precedents in their every act.

They were both male and female, Buchtel being among the very few colleges of its day to be coeducational from inception. Those in the collegiate program were traditional college-age students; the "preps" (those in the preparatory department) were of high school age or younger. Most came from rural and small town backgrounds, and most were from Ohio, although they represented a geographic spread from Vermont in the east to Kansas in the west.

A pair of Vermont farm boys, Charlie and Fred Parmenter, were first to arrive on campus. President McCollester and the president of the Board, John R. Buchtel, welcomed them and the other new arrivals. Fred soon reported to his parents that "Mr. Buchtel is a jolly good fellow. He is full of fun and always seems to be happy as a clam in high water. He has invited us to come down to his house and get all the apples and grapes we wanted." A few weeks later Fred reported that "We went out to Copla [Copley] swamp with the President of the college and Mr. Buchtel to shoot pigeons. We got eight pigeons and a squirrel and was only gone from here three hours and it is four miles out there." At least one of the two presidents also personally served *in loco parentis* when the need arose. When Fred was feeling "poorly," President McCollester told him to exercise and later brought him a medicine he had prepared. "By the way," Fred reassured his parents, "he is a pretty good physician as well as a minister."

Many of the students in the preparatory department were very young to be living away from home in an enormous building with older students. Though they were constantly under the vigilant eye of the faculty, they greatly needed comfort and support. Vincent Tomlinson, for example, was only ten years old when he arrived at Buchtel College. It is not surprising, therefore, that the most lasting impression of his first year was the exhuming of bodies from graves of the cemetery the campus had once been. One can well imagine the little boy's difficulty in going to sleep in the great, dark building.

In the beginning the faculty had certain reservations about the capabilities of the College's female students. At the 1874 commencement ceremony, Sara Smelzer and Anna Fleming committed their essays to memory so that they would not have to hold their manuscripts when it came their turn to perform. But, said those in charge, only boys could deliver "orations," and they insisted that the girls hold their manuscripts. The two girls refused, and each flawlessly recited her essay from memory. This show of independence so pleased John R. Buchtel that he gave them each $25—at a time when tuition for the entire year was $30. Whatever preconceptions may have remained, the 1878 catalog noted that the college was open alike to students of both sexes and that all were admitted to equal privileges and honors. "The results achieved in Buchtel College," it read, "testify to the ability of the young ladies to compete successfully with the young gentlemen for the prizes of scholarship. . . . The influences exerted by the sexes upon each other have been wholly beneficial."

Buchtel in its first years was a "country college." Students were largely of rural and small town origins, and many were lacking in social graces. A student of that time wrote that opportunities for social development were especially favorable because Buchtel was small enough for each student's social shortcomings to be noted by professors and fellow students, who would then assist or ridicule the student into socially acceptable conduct.

Ridicule as a form of social training did not always work. Henry Morris of Chicago responded so poorly to being tossed in a blanket, a common form of hazing, that he had his tormentors arrested. Thereafter he found it expedient to hire a bodyguard to escort him to campus functions. His difficulties increased, and he withdrew from school. Twenty-five years later, however, after a successful career as United States Consul in Ghent, Belgium, and as a successful attorney in Washington, D.C., he was awarded an honorary Master's degree from Buchtel College. He responded by bequeathing 20,000 volumes to the College library, where his gift still forms an important part of the collection.

The college dance was another vehicle of social training. It may be, as the catalog claimed, that the "influences ex-

erted by the sexes upon each other have been wholly beneficial," but there were limits. In square dances boys
danced with girls, but in round dances boys danced with
boys and girls with girls. As one participant later recalled,
"Whoever said that dancing is . . . poetry [in] motion
never saw two men trying to waltz or polka together in
the basement of Buchtel." The faculty, he continued, "sat
in one corner of the room, in icy and lofty seclusion, and
eyed us ominously. I think they feared that under the sin-
compelling influence of the dance we would lead some
husky partner to a bar and buy him a drink."

As the college matured, students found expanding opportunities for entertainment, some in student organizations on campus, others in Akron and its surrounding
countryside. By the end of the nineteenth century con-
certs, operettas, minstrel shows, and dramas featuring
some of the nation's foremost performers came to local
theaters on regular rotation. For outdoor diversion, the
many lakes, the beautiful scenery of the Cuyahoga Gorge
with its Fosdick's Inn featuring chicken and hot biscuit
dinners, the popular Gaylord's Grove picnic grounds, the
attractions of boating on the Cuyahoga River or dancing
in the pavilion at Silver Lake, the fish fries at State Mill
and the outings to Young's Hotel, the chestnut groves and
sugar camps, all added to the charm of college life.

Buchtel College grew during the late Victorian period,
a time when proper conduct and sex roles were carefully
spelled out. Universalists, like most Protestants, regarded
such overt signs of weakness as smoking, drinking, swear-
ing, and failure to attend Sunday services as cause for
concern if not alarm. The College minimized chances for
deviant behavior by requiring every candidate for admis-

motivated student to learn some German, with Professor Carl Kolbe driving him on in daily recitations, than it would be for today's student of similar talents and motivation to learn a language from tapes in the language laboratory. Perhaps the most difficult problem students face today is to do what they should, when they should. Independent study requires the student to be a self-starter; that was an alien idea at Buchtel College.

In the early years Buchtel students dealt only with texts and recitations. A member of the class of 1880 declared: "We were rarely encouraged to go outside of the textbook; and no collateral reading was either required or suggested. We were not urged to use the library; indeed, it might be asserted that any utilization of its few books was almost discouraged. I for one never climbed its stairs to avail myself of its carefully guarded treasure, and I doubt if any of my classmates was more daring in adventuring . . . within its austere walls, lined with glazed cases all cautiously locked."

Students who completed college in the late nineteenth century belonged to an intellectual and cultural elite, and often to a financial one as well. But many who later enjoyed successful careers had to work their way through school. Tom Prior, who slopped President McCollester's hogs for tuition money, was the precursor of today's student who works to earn money for college expenses. Many students reduced costs by rooming and boarding in nearby homes rather than paying the higher costs of dormitory living. Prominent among the landladies was Mrs. Lucinda "Aunty" Brown, who ran student boardinghouses for over thirty years. Her first boardinghouse, located on Carroll Street, was nicknamed the Old Shoe; she later moved to a larger house called the New Shoe. Generations of Buchtel students remembered her affectionately.

To a substantial degree the College was a self-contained community. There was little contact at first between the students and city kids or "townies," but after a time interaction between the groups increased. An ever-growing proportion of the student body was composed of local students, most of whom were not from Universalist families. Fraternities rented rooms in the city; sororities often held parties at members' homes in Akron; students and townspeople mingled in local churches; and the College's baseball nine played local teams. Yet local people continued to see Buchtel College as a thing apart. Not until Buchtel became the locally supported municipal university was the emotional gulf separating town and gown finally bridged.

By the time Buchtel College lost its identity within The Municipal University of Akron it had awarded 465 baccalaureate degrees, an average of eleven per year. Of these 248 were granted to men and 217 to women. Although the College produced no president of the nation, governor, Supreme Court justice, or Nobel Laureate, it did produce a talented and competent group of professionals in medicine, law, teaching, politics, nursing, agriculture, finance, journalism, scientific research, the ministry, the arts, business enterprise, and all sorts of public service. It was a worthy achievement.

7

The Women of Old Buchtel

rom its inception, Buchtel College welcomed women on an equal basis with men. Although founded more than three decades after Oberlin College established the precedent, Buchtel was among the minority of American coeducational schools. At the cornerstone-laying of July 4, 1871, John R. Buchtel had set the tone when he reminded his audience that the new college would qualify men for work, "and *women too*," and the women were to be on equal terms with the men.

The liberal element within Universalism had traditionally supported women's rights. One mark of their sincerity was the practice of ordaining women for the ministry at a time when virtually no other denomination would consider doing so. Another mark was their determination to have women enter fully into the life of the College.

Each year the College's president presented the Ohio Universalist Convention with a report on student deportment and the moral tone on campus. The reports were uniformly optimistic, assuring the Convention that Buchtel was the equal of its sister institutions in protecting and improving the morals of its charges.

Monitoring the moral climate was easier than it was to become in later decades. Americans adhered to a Judeo-Christian ethical structure that was constantly reinforced by family, church, and school. The confusion in values that arose after World War I was still well in the future, and the latitudinarian practices of post–World War II America would have been shocking beyond belief. One threat to women students came from a state requirement that external fire escapes be erected at Buchtel Hall. Keeping males off the ladders proved difficult. Despite the posting of a guard, the girls were bothered by a "ghost," a neighborhood adventurer, a faculty member visiting a coed, and assorted other climbers. (One suspects, although it was never suggested in College records, that some of this attention may have been encouraged.)

College women enjoyed a variety of social activities. In addition to dances, class socials, and the like, a literary society was organized from the first. Named the Cary Society in honor of Alice and Phoebe Cary, Ohio sisters who had gained a national reputation for their verse, the society later split into the Alice Society and the Phoebe Society when the older members wanted to distance themselves from the younger ones. Sororities soon appeared: Kappa Kappa Gamma in 1877 and Delta Gamma in 1879. Meeting rooms were provided in West Hall. Local members sometimes invited their "sisters" to dinners or entertainments held in their Akron homes. Early in the twentieth century sororities and other women's groups became more venturesome, taking launch trips via the Ohio Canal to Long Lake and visiting local picnic groves.

The destruction of Buchtel Hall in 1899 eliminated dormitory life except for a handful of women who were accommodated in a nearby temporary dormitory called Masaldwar, and later in Curtis Cottage, erected on campus in 1905. As more women lived at home in Akron and vicinity, some of the early closeness among the College women was lost.

Another dimension to the women's role was provided by female faculty members, of whom Buchtel at one time or another had more than fifty. They dominated instruction in English, history, rhetoric (speech), art, and music, and several had duties now assigned to department heads. No woman held College administrative office, but Abby Soule Schumacher (1892–97) and Henrietta G. Moore (1893–1900) served as Trustees. Women faculty members provided the students with examples of careers outside the traditional confines of the home. Within the constraints of late Victorian sex roles, they exhibited an unaccustomed degree of independence and self-reliance.

One such liberated faculty member was Mary Jewett, the daughter of an Akron physician. Following her graduation from Buchtel in 1876, she taught at Hiram College before returning to her alma mater to take the chair of English literature. One of the first Buchtel graduates to be appointed to the faculty, she was known for her affable manner and keen enthusiasm for her students. She resigned in 1892 and spent the next eighteen years in New York City in medical study and practice, working in public health clinics serving the city's poor and dispossessed. In 1910 she left medical practice and relocated in Winter Haven, Florida. There, as she reported, she turned into "a Florida cracker, farmer, fruit grower, and in some small way, a social worker."

Other women faculty members made strong contributions to the College in its early years. Dora Merrill, bright, lively, effective in her teaching, was the first to teach history as a separate subject. She resigned in 1892 and became manager of "several hundred acres" of apple orchards and farms in Emmett, Idaho. Jennie Gifford, principal of the preparatory school and teacher in the normal course, was also a strong personality. One of her successors, Martha Bortle, of "commanding presence and happy temperament," was an ordained minister of the Universalist faith and later became pastor of the Universalist church in Hamilton, Ohio.

Women such as these were influential in preparing

8

At the Heart
of the Enterprise

he grand new College building was not yet complete on September 11, 1872, when Carl F. Kolbe held his recitation in German—the first class to meet in Buchtel College. The presence of Professor Kolbe on the faculty can be traced to John R. Buchtel, who was instrumental both in employing new faculty members and in helping them feel at ease. Thirty years after meeting this first class, Kolbe recalled how Buchtel eased him into the new College community by introducing him as follows to President McCollester and the Board of Trustees: "Now gentlemen, this is the man who is going to teach our girls and boys Dutch; and I think he is the right man."

Kolbe was indeed the right man, but it was a struggle, then as now, to sign up and retain people who could bring talent and dedication to teaching and scholarly activities. In the College's early days, faculty members were conspicuous; there were only eight of them initially, and only fifteen in the collegiate department in 1913 when Buchtel College was transformed into The Municipal University of

Akron. Their work was highly visible; any temperamental or pedagogic shortcomings, supposed or real, were readily spotted and commented upon. Three members of that first faculty were fired at the end of the first year, for the Trustees were quick to release professors who failed to measure up personally or professionally.

The life and duties of faculty members have changed remarkably since 1872. In that year, eight people—including President McCollester, who doubled as Professor of Intellectual and Moral Philosophy—had to teach 46 college students and 171 preparatory students. In 1879 President Rexford created separate faculties for the collegiate and preparatory departments, and henceforth the collegiate classes were small. In most subjects the professor met the class to hear students recite class assignments, many of which were of considerable length. Teachers were expected to be on duty throughout the day. Although there is now no way of determining their teaching load, as recently as 1916 the "term hour load" for professors was eighteen hours, to be reduced to sixteen hours as soon as conditions permitted. Present teaching loads are modest in comparison, but now faculty serve much larger numbers of students in courses that are far more diverse in structure and comprehensive in coverage than the recitation-oriented courses of an earlier time.

Buchtel College faculty members had many responsibilities that were later turned over to administrative officers. They made up class schedules, supervised the curriculum, and enforced discipline. Until 1922 most of these duties were carried out by the faculty as a whole; but by that year the general faculty, now nearly 50 members, was too big to do business any longer as a committee of the whole.

Accordingly a general university faculty council with an executive committee was formed, as were separate faculties for the college of liberal arts, the college of engineering and commerce, the teacher's college, and the evening session.

As for discipline, one may be sure that the current faculty would not welcome the burden of monitoring and chaperoning student manners that fell to their predecessors. To make the faculty even more available for these purposes, the Board directed in 1880 that male faculty members not having families should live and take their meals in the College building. On some disciplinary matters the faculty passed the buck to the Board. Thus when two young gentlemen were found locked in the "sleeping apartment" of a female student, "certain grave questions growing out of this circumstance were referred to the Board." The judgment of those solons is not recorded.

Many faculty members were regarded with genuine respect and affection by their students and colleagues. Among them was Kolbe, whom students irreverently referred to as "Umlaut" and who later was called "Buchtel's most perfect gentleman." In his classes he requested that the young ladies and gentlemen "not sit mixed"; but mixed or not, all agreed they learned German. Kolbe died in May 1905, on a Wednesday; the college buildings were draped in black, and all work was suspended for the rest of the week. It is difficult to imagine that the passing of any professor in this day would elicit such an intense reaction.

Some of the most memorable faculty members served Buchtel in its waning days and continued to serve the new municipal university with distinction. Among them was a young man from Leroy, Ohio, named Hezzleton Erastus Simmons, whom we shall meet again when, after a long career as professor of chemistry with side excursions into administrative posts, he emerged in 1933 as president of The University of Akron. Albert Spanton, Simmons's contemporary, became a much admired professor of English and rhetoric in 1905 after serving an apprenticeship in the preparatory program. Former students remembered with affection, amusement, or embarrassment their portrayals of Shakespearian characters in his classroom, as when a sobersides read Falstaff or a brawny football player enunciated Romeo's appeals to Juliet. This technique may appear better calculated to amuse than to instruct, but the students who experienced this treatment remembered more than their temporary discomfiture; they remembered something of Shakespeare, and of Spanton.

In the 1920s and 1930s, as dean of the Buchtel college of liberal arts, Spanton earned respect as "the Little Dean" (he was barely five feet tall). His successor as dean was Charles Bulger, professor of German and another carryover from Buchtel College days. Like Simmons and Spanton, Bulger handled a number of administrative activities in addition to teaching German language and literature. One noteworthy early contribution of his was to take charge of Buchtel's chaotic, student-run athletic program as faculty manager and bring order to the effort, thus saving the College much embarrassment.

Buchtel's faculty was a teaching faculty, yet there were those who earned acclaim through research and scholarly accomplishment. The best example was Charles M. Knight, the creator of college courses in rubber chemistry. Hezzleton Simmons, his student and later successor, was followed in more recent times by G. Stafford Whitby, a world authority in the field. Their work in rubber chemistry expanded after World War II into the world-renowned Institute of Polymer Science under Maurice Morton, assisted by Alan Gent, James Harwood, and their associates. Today's College of Polymer Science and Polymer Engineering, the first of its kind in the nation, maintains Akron's international stature in the field.

How did teachers fare economically? In the beginning the College offered salaries adequate to attract and keep talented teachers, but the 1890s brought hard times. John R. Buchtel's death in 1892 and the prolonged 1890s depression forced a 10 to 20 percent salary cut in 1895 and another 10 percent cut in 1897. Several teaching positions were consolidated or abolished, and in 1898 the highest professor's salary was $1,400.

Salary levels were still minimal when the City of Akron took over operation of the College in 1913. That change made it possible for President Parke R. Kolbe to raise salaries substantially two years in a row, which caused the *Akron Beacon Journal* to complain editorially about "the high cost of professors" and to charge that President Kolbe had "whooped up" professors' salaries as soon as he knew that the city was to pay the bill. Salaries failed to keep pace with inflation during World War I, however, and in 1919 every member of the faculty signed a petition to the Board requesting a 30 percent salary increase. The Board granted an increase of $300 across the board, a substantial boost though less than the faculty had requested. That petition having worked so well, the faculty the next year petitioned for $400 across the board, but the Board took no action because a business recession had reduced tax revenues.

Salaries then improved slowly until after the onset of the Great Depression; in October 1931 they were reduced 10 percent and the following April an additional 10 to 25 percent. Soon afterward faculty and staff were paid in scrip. On July 1, 1932, indefinite tenure was suspended and faculty members were placed on month-to-month appointment. Although tenure was reinstated in 1937, the first general faculty salary increase following the Depression was delayed until 1941. After World War II the faculty again petitioned for salary increases, but received little satisfaction. When President Norman P. Auburn arrived in 1951, he found that the highest-paid faculty member, a professor with over 40 years' service, was paid just over $5,000. Auburn promptly made faculty salary development a high priority of his administration.

Finally, a word about teaching. What is it that makes a teacher great? There seems to be no formula. The range of variables is illustrated by two men, near polar opposites, each of whom was regarded on the Akron campus as a "great" teacher.

One was Oscar E. Olin, who served as principal of the preparatory school from 1898 to 1904, at which time he became professor of economics and history and instructor in mental and moral philosophy. Until 1914 he taught all that the College had to offer in history, logic, psychology, philosophy, and the social sciences. The other was Summerfield Baldwin, III, who from his arrival on campus during World War II until his death in 1955 served as professor of history and head of the department.

9

Lucius V. Bierce,
First Friend of the Library

It is a truism that fame is fleeting. Vital, energetic persons soon pass from mind, and efforts to preserve their memory lose force as years pass. So it is with Lucius V. Bierce. Consider Bierce Library! Faculty and students walk by it, use its facilities, and check out its books daily without giving a thought to its name. Yet a century and a half ago Lucius Verus Bierce was Akron's most colorful citizen, known especially for his audacious invasion of Canada.

On the dark night of December 3, 1838, General Bierce of Akron (he was a general in the Ohio militia) led a motley band of 137 adventurers to the Detroit waterfront, where they seized a steamship. Eluding U.S. patrol boats on the Detroit River, they landed on the Canadian shore about three miles upstream from the little town of Windsor. The rowdy troop quickly attacked the town, routed the tiny garrison guarding it, burned a Canadian steamship, and then took up defensive positions. A British army surgeon, one Major Hume, blundered into their lines and was killed while scouting out the invaders. His sword was presented to Bierce as commanding officer. Hours later Canadian militia attacked and captured all but about thirty of the invaders. Captured officers were hanged; other prisoners were sent to a British penal colony in Tasmania.

Bierce was among the two dozen or so who escaped. He led the survivors to the Windsor waterfront, where they stole boats, and, using their gun butts as paddles, crossed the Detroit River to safety on the American shore. Thus ended a bizarre attempt by the Hunters, an American secret society, to help rebels liberate Canada from British control, an attempt occasioned by the Canadian Rebellion of 1837. For many years after this fiasco, Bierce, styled the "Hero of Windsor" by his admirers, lived with a price on his head. No one claimed it, however, and two efforts to prosecute him in federal court for violating United States neutrality laws also proved unsuccessful. Indeed, shortly after returning to his Akron residence, Bierce was elected mayor of the town. In years to come he would be elected to that office three more times.

Who was Lucius Verus Bierce? Born in 1801 in Cornwall Bridge, Connecticut, he was one of eleven children of William Bierce, a shoemaker, hardscrabble farmer, and veteran of the Revolutionary armies. William must have had some education, for he named one of his sons Marcus Aurelius after the famous Roman emperor and sage. Marcus Aurelius Bierce, incidentally, became the father of Ambrose Bierce, sometimes called "Bitter Bierce," a famous late-nineteenth-century American writer of Civil War stories and of the bitingly sarcastic *Devil's Dictionary*. Some say he modeled himself and his prose style on his uncle Lucius.

In 1817, following the death of his wife, William Bierce brought his family to Nelson Township, Portage County, in Ohio's Western Reserve. That same year Lucius walked to Athens, Ohio, to enter Ohio University, then little more than a secondary school. The desperately poor, raw young student matured along with the school, and his B.A. degree, awarded in 1822, placed him among the first graduates of an Ohio college. The skills he learned in debates sponsored by his literary society, the Athenians, served him well throughout life.

Had Bierce been a wealthy young man he might well have taken the Grand Tour of European castles, literary shrines, and battlefields so common to graduates of that day. Being poor, however, he did the next best thing. In company with a college companion, he set out on a walking trip through the upper South. In Charleston, Virginia (now West Virginia), he saw slavery at first hand, and the sight totally unnerved him: "I blushed that I was an American, and cursed the land that could thus traffic in human flesh." In the Carolinas and Georgia he passed through Cherokee lands and the Creek Nation, observing the hard lot of the American Indian, the evils of miscegenation, and the rapacity of whites appropriating Indian lands. Twice along the way Bierce stopped for an extended stay: first in South Carolina, where he taught school for six weeks, and then in northern Alabama, where he read law for several months, long enough to gain admission to the Alabama bar. In 1823 he ended his 1,800-mile trek by returning to Ohio, and years later he recorded an account of his trip in a travel journal still in the possession of Bierce Library.

Once back in Ohio, Bierce resumed reading law to qualify for practice before the Ohio bar, to which he was admitted in 1825. He established his practice in Ravenna, the seat of Portage County, and his neighbors promptly elected him prosecuting attorney. As prosecutor he tried to eliminate a gang of counterfeiters who practiced their craft in the Cuyahoga Valley, about twelve miles north of Akron. Led by Jim Brown and his brother Dan, this gang became one of the largest and boldest in the nation. They were wholesalers of "queer," leaving it to the retailers (tavern keepers, livery stable operators, and others) to get caught passing the fake money.

Bierce figured in an unusual way in the gang's greatest scheme. The Browns and their confederates went to New Orleans, bought a ship with counterfeit funds, put their printing press, their supplies, and their engraver on board, and prepared to sail for China and other distant places. There they intended to use counterfeit bills to purchase trade goods, which they would then sell in world ports for legitimate money. The night before they were to sail, a suspicious constable discovered their plans, and the plotters ended up in a New Orleans jail. Jim Brown wrote to his wife back in Boston, Ohio, urging her to employ the best criminal lawyers available to get them out of jail. She promptly hired Bierce and an associate to do the job, and they succeeded. Though Dan Brown died in jail, Jim was freed. He returned, and his friends along the Ohio-Erie Canal promptly elected him Justice of the Peace. If that seems a little strange, it is also strange to non-lawyers that Lucius Bierce, the man who was trying to put the Browns in jail in Portage County, Ohio, should take a fee to spring them from jail in New Orleans.

As his career flourished, Bierce decided to move to Akron, a new canal and industrial town that promised to outstrip Ravenna. The human flotsam and jetsam of canal

men along the banks of Ossawatomie Creek in eastern
Kansas, where they murdered five proslavery men in cold
blood. Among their weapons were short swords presumably left over from Bierce's abortive raid on Windsor.
Bierce admitted that he had helped Brown, and it seems
likely that he also supplied money and/or arms for Brown's
more famous raid on Harper's Ferry, Virginia, in 1859. On
the day Brown was hanged in Charles Town, Virginia (December 2, 1859), Bierce told an Akron audience: "It is said
'Old Brown was crazy.' Would to God we had millions of
such crazy men [in] the North, who were willing to peril
life for right and universal liberty." He closed his speech
by lamenting the passing of "our old friend and neighbor,
John Brown."

Bierce tried to enlist in the Union army after South Carolina forces fired on Fort Sumter in April 1861. Bitterly
disappointed to learn that at age 60 he was too old for
military service, the General did the next best thing. At
his own expense he recruited two companies of marines
and transported them to the Washington Navy Yard. Later
he raised a company of 100 soldiers and paid them out of
his own pocket. He worked endlessly to encourage en-
listments and won election to the Ohio senate, where he
supported every pro-war initiative. In 1863 he was finally
permitted to enlist in the Ohio Volunteers as a major, with
duties as an assistant adjutant general. At the end of the
war he commanded two midwestern camps during their
decommissioning, expending over one million dollars in
public money and accounting for every cent.

Throughout his busy life, Lucius Bierce retained an interest in history and scholarship. In addition to a transla-
tion of Seneca's *Morals*, he published *Historical Reminis-*

cences of Summit County (1854), the first published history of the county, and other historical pieces in regional newspapers and journals. Woe to anyone rash enough to challenge the General's version of events; a self-righteous tirade greeted all who tried.

Toward the end of his life Bierce took refuge in his studies and in Masonic activities. He remained keenly interested in his rapidly growing city, and few things pleased him more than the chartering of Buchtel College. Having bequeathed his homesite to the city to be used as a public park (the city later used it as the site of the Carnegie library), he now determined to leave his personal library, his fossil collection, his presidential autograph collection, the sword captured from Major Hume, and other artifacts to the new Universalist school on Spicer Hill. He also donated $5,000 for book purchases, and in appreciation the Trustees named the library in his honor. That library and its collections were destroyed in the 1899 fire.

For sixteen years following the fire there was no separate library facility on campus. In 1916, however, The Municipal University of Akron dedicated Carl F. Kolbe Hall, an Italianate red-brick structure that housed a collection once more known as Bierce Library. Carl Kolbe Hall was razed in the 1950s to make room for an expanded collection in a new building then called simply University Library. When the present library building was constructed in the 1970s, it was to be named the University Library and Learning Resources Center; but that bland name proved to have few supporters and history professor Don R. Gerlach led a movement to preserve Bierce's name. With the Trustees' blessing, it was done.

Lucius Bierce died in 1876, the nation's centennial year. His contributions to city, state, and nation were profound. He was not always a comfortable man to be around, for he held strong convictions and asserted them with vigor. But he was the implacable foe of meanness and injustice. "To those who partially knew him," said his former law partner, General Alvin Coe Voris, "he was full of antitheses." But to those who knew him best, "he was a noble specimen of his race—eminently a man of conviction and heart."

One likes to think that this friend of the young, this fervent advocate of learning, would be pleased to know that Bierce Library stands today at the center of the University's scholarly enterprise, and that the seed he planted more than a century ago has borne a mighty harvest.

10

Buchtel College and Intercollegiate Athletics

t did not take the Buchtel College boys long to organize their first athletic contest. On October 5, 1872, the College's baseball nine played a team from the city, and the first intercollegiate athletic contest in Akron took place the following year. The baseball team of 1873 played three games with other colleges and one each with an Akron nine and one from Cuyahoga Falls. They won just one of the five games, beating Wooster 38–20. Not until 1879 would they again play more than one game a year; indeed they did not win another baseball game until beating Wooster 22–6 that year.

The games were played on vacant lots across Carroll Street from the campus. Money to purchase bats and balls was obtained by passing the hat. Baseballs were so scarce that play had to be halted whenever the ball was lost in weeds or puddles. Of course, these first baseball games were entirely a student undertaking: the players made their own arrangements and paid their own expenses.

In 1890 representatives from Buchtel met with their

counterparts from Wooster, Denison, and Ohio State at the Arcade Hotel in Springfield and agreed to form the Ohio Inter-Collegiate Athletic Association. Only a bona fide student could compete, that is, one who had "attended at least two college exercises for two weeks prior to the date of the contest." The latitude afforded by this definition hampered no one seriously, and "ringers" (non-students) continued to play on college teams.

Football made its appearance in 1891. Sandlot games were played prior to that time, but the advent of the Athletic Association gave impetus to the formation of a College team. Buchtel's new team lost to Western Reserve Academy 22–6 at Hudson. On November 5, 1891, Kenyon came to Akron to play the city's first intercollegiate football game, defeating Buchtel 42–0.

Buchtel athletics received a big boost with the completion of Crouse Gymnasium in 1888 and the development of Buchtel Field in 1892. The field was located four blocks south of the campus at the corner of Kling and Wheeler Streets. A running track and tennis courts were part of the facility, and the entire area was fenced in. The new athletic grounds were opened October 15, 1892, on the day of the first football game of the season. The College band paraded through Akron's streets followed by the Buchtel and Case teams in wagons. The Buchtel fans had less reason to cheer after the game started as Case scored a 14–9 victory.

It was apparent that if Buchtel were to hold its own with other colleges, the team must have a coach. The 1892 team was assisted by a Mr. Cook from the Cleveland Athletic Club, and his advice helped make possible victories over Denison and Hiram and over the Akron Athletic Club in the first Thanksgiving Day game in Akron's history. But the boys sought a permanent director of athletics. With President Cone's blessing and his promise to arrange for the Board of Trustees to pay the director's salary, the boys sought out John W. Heisman, a recent graduate of the University of Pennsylvania, who had coached the undefeated Oberlin football team of 1892. Heisman accepted Buchtel's offer and soon set about coaching the baseball and football teams of 1893.

The coach's job was far from easy. Buchtel had about 100 boys, a number of whom worked their way through school, so there were scarcely enough to field a team and almost no scrubs to practice against. The editor of the *Buchtelite* lent his support by urging "someone to sacrifice himself for the good of his fellow students and for his college." Just the way he said it had an ominous ring.

Under these handicaps Coach Heisman's success, especially with the football team, was remarkable. His 1893 team enjoyed instant success, winning five of its seven games and outscoring its opponents 276 to 82. One of the defeats, however, was a galling 32–18 loss to Ohio State. Buchtel craved revenge.

As the 1894 season approached, promoters of the Ohio State Fair in Columbus decided to boost attendance by staging a football tournament matching Ohio State against Buchtel, Denison, and Wittenberg successively. The games were played in September on a gridiron that had been laid out inside the racetrack oval. A newspaper reporter assured his readers that aside from the presence of "many stubbles" in the field, it was a "very desirable spot" for the contests. The "stubbles" could be troublesome, however. A Buchtel player explained why: "It was the fashion

then for the man with the ball to keep on crawling with
twenty-one men, more or less, on top of him, as the ball
was not 'down' so long as in motion. The only effective
way to stop crawling was to jump on the fellow's head
and ram his face into the ground."

Buchtel's team was in excellent condition and anxious
to square accounts with Ohio State. Much of Buchtel's
strength, as it happened, was due to the presence of Heisman himself at quarterback, and Ohio State was also
charged with using ringers.

The game was exciting. Buchtel's favorite play was to
attack the end of Ohio's line and, being blocked, to turn
the charge into a mass play aimed at the tackle position.
The play "invariably made . . . good gains." Though Ohio's
men played well, their teamwork showed "poor training,"
and at the end of the twenty-minute first half the score
was 6–6. The second half was scoreless as a Heisman fum-
ble on Ohio's two-yard line kept Buchtel from the winning
score. A sudden-death overtime period followed after a
ten-minute rest period, scarcely long enough to overcome
a fatigue intensified by heat and by dust from horse races
run while the game was in progress.

Many years later, John Heisman recalled the details of
that overtime period. Buchtel battered its way to Ohio's
four-yard line while sparing its fullback, Frank Fisher, who
was "seeing things" from the heat and the battering he
had absorbed. Heisman rallied his men with a pep talk
designed to inspire one last effort, and then called for
Fisher to buck through Ohio's right tackle. As Heisman
later explained:

I got hold of the ball safely and stuck it squarely in his bread-
basket. Fortunately he either saw or felt it—and got it. Then

away we all went like mad. I think about every man on the team
had his hands on Frank somewhere, for . . . hiking the runner
was *the* big thing in the game. I recall I had hold of him by the
back of his jersey and was going in front of him. And we all
went through together, just like the water of a mill-dam when
the dam goes out. With a last yank I tore the jersey clear off
Frank's back—but what did it matter since we were across.

The pleasure of this 12–6 victory was undercut by the
Buchtel faculty, which informed the coach that sports
would hereafter be for the benefit of "the regular students
of the college," in order "to minister to the physical development of those engaged in this exercise." His contract
canceled, Heisman left Buchtel for greener fields at Georgia Tech and Auburn, where he won enduring fame in
football annals. Today the Heisman Trophy is awarded
annually to the nation's top collegiate player. Buchtel re-

turned to simon-pure amateurism and a string of unsuccessful seasons.

The loss of Heisman and the collapse of the newborn
Ohio Inter-Collegiate Athletic Association after the 1893
season dampened students' enthusiasm for athletics. The
editor of the *Buchtelite*, disgusted with the lack of interest,
urged male students to give a little time to athletics instead
of "talking with the girls in the library, lounging in each
other's rooms and running to cheap third class theatres."
Not only baseball and football were affected. Tennis, track,
and fencing had each made an appearance on Buchtel's
athletic scene, but no sustained effort was made in any of
these sports at that time.

In 1901 a new Athletic Association was formed by Buchtel students. The Association's board of directors supervised the scheduling of games and passed on all expen-
ditures. Any faculty member, student, or alumnus could
be a member of the Association, and every member of an
athletic team was required to be. In response to a student
petition, the Trustees increased the student incidental fee
by one dollar to support the Association. In 1902 the faculty adopted an eligibility rule requiring an athlete to be
passing at least eight hours of work and attending class
regularly. Some members of the 1903 basketball team were
unable to meet even this simple test and were declared
ineligible, much to the disgust of student sports enthusiasts. Protests could not move Joseph Rockwell, chairman
of the faculty committee on athletics, and a "much needed
step forward was taken in control of athletics."

In football the dreary story was "no team" owing to

"lack of interest," "not enough men in the College," or even "parental objections." Another problem was the irresponsibility displayed by students charged with managing the finances of athletic teams. Year after year the College was embarrassed by unpaid bills resulting from student managers' carelessness or indifference to their responsibilities. Finally the faculty cracked down, voting in 1908 "that further intercollegiate athletics be suspended until the deficit in basketball and the probable deficit in baseball be provided for, and that the financial condition of athletics at Buchtel be put before the Student Council for adjustment."

A committee composed of local alumni members of the Board of Trustees conducted an investigation, held open meetings with students, and then recommended that a coach be hired for the coming year. In March 1909 the Trustees voted to hire a director of physical training and athletic coach who would also be a faculty member. This position was filled by Clarence Weed, who brought order to Buchtel's athletic efforts though he stayed just a year.

With the hiring of Frank Haggerty as coach in 1910 three ingredients essential to a successful program—permanent organization, funds, and professional coaching—were finally put together. While Haggerty took care of the coaching, organizational work was entrusted to Charles Bulger, a young professor of German who in 1910 became faculty manager of athletics as well. He assumed control over scheduling and the handling of funds, greatly improving Buchtel's performance in this respect. In 1915 Fred Sefton came to Akron as director of physical training, and also replaced Bulger as faculty manager of athletics. In this combined capacity he performed the activities that are now the province of the director of athletics and the head of the physical education department.

Basketball was introduced as a varsity sport by Charles Knight, who had seen it played in the East. It was taken up first by the girls of the academy and then by the academy boys, who organized the first team in 1901. Intercollegiate competition started in 1902, when the Buchtel neophytes went up against an experienced Mount Union team and lost 120–9—in a day when a good team might score only 30 points in a game! The local boys were fast learners, however, and the 1904 season was spectacular, with Mount Union, Western Reserve, Hiram, West Virginia University, and Indiana University all falling before the Buchtel onslaught. But the zenith of Buchtel's early basketball experiences was a victory over Yale on New Year's Day, 1908.

Yale, a national power in those days, offered to play Buchtel if it was guaranteed $200. Team captain Charles Jahant and student manager Lucien King secured permission from the faculty to accept the offer and then promoted the game so successfully that every seat in Crouse Gym was sold out at reserved-seat prices. The game was all the spectators had paid for, a hard-fought contest that the unknown Buchtel team won 36–30 over its famed opponents. It was a great day for Old Buchtel, its memory scarcely dimmed by Yale's 32–28 revenge victory the next year.

Buchtel teams often played nationally prominent teams in those years. The 1910 football team won seven of its nine games, but one of the defeats was 51–0 to Notre Dame. Buchtel never made the mistake of playing Notre Dame again, but it took successive defeats—41–0 in 1913 and 75–6 in 1914—by the Michigan Aggies (now the Michigan State Spartans) to convince the local boys that it made more sense to play teams from smaller schools. Not until the late 1930s would another attempt be made to run in fast football company.

Intercollegiate athletics reached maturity in 1915, when The Municipal University of Akron found a proper home in the Ohio Athletic Conference, in which it remained (with a brief hiatus in the 1930s) for the next 52 years.

11

Buchtel College Becomes
The Municipal
University of Akron

ew things cling so tenaciously to life as an institution determined to fulfill its mission. When one reads of Buchtel's mounting financial problems, notably the death of its principal financial backers and the costs resulting from the 1899 fire, it is clear that the College faced a fundamental choice after 1900: adjust or die. As the financial crisis deepened, Buchtel Trustees urged Lombard College, a faltering Universalist college in Galesburg, Illinois, to consider a merger. Lombard chose to go it alone, however, and was ultimately forced to close.

Buchtel had another alternative. The ashes of Old Buchtel had scarcely cooled before suggestions were made for refinancing the College and relocating the campus. Professor Samuel P. Orth, serving on a committee to plan Buchtel's rebuilding, suggested that a new campus be built on city-owned land west of the city proper. No record remains of the reaction to this proposal. Next he investigated the possibility of obtaining city tax support for the

College, but local attorneys told him it would take a special act of the legislature and the idea was dropped.

Between 1900, when this idea was put forward, and 1913, when city tax support was finally obtained, Buchtel's financial plight became ever more pronounced. According to a Buchtel alumna, the community during this period "took the College for granted, smiling benevolently over its prosperity, but apparently not appreciating its times of adversity."

During this same thirteen-year period, Akron was being transformed from a modest-sized city of diversified industry to a large industrial city dominated by the flourishing rubber industry. In 1900 Akron had about 45,000 residents. The population swelled to 70,000 by 1910 and by 1913 had reached about 100,000 as trainloads of workers, recruited by factory representatives and lured by excellent wages, arrived from Pennsylvania, the Appalachian regions of Ohio and neighboring states, and overseas. Akron was no longer the well-ordered town that had appealed to nineteenth-century visitors. Jerry-built structures popped up in unlikely places; houses were rushed to completion on tiny lots scarcely large enough for a garage; there were shortages of everything—schools, parks, transportation. The newcomers had no ties to Akron. Many were single young men who spent their money on food, drink, entertainment, and expensive clothing, especially silk shirts, which were the rubberworker's badge of affluence. For those whose roots were in the country, the city was an alien place. They felt no loyalty to it; indeed, many expected to make money quickly and then return home, where people were "real folks."

As President A. B. Church fought to keep Buchtel alive,

he must have longed for assistance from the economically booming city. At least we know that he had a plan "long in thought." After Church's premature death in November 1912, the presidency of Buchtel devolved upon Parke R. Kolbe, who assumed office in February 1913. His wife, Lydia Voris Kolbe, recalled that Kolbe, not quite 32 years of age, accepted the appointment with equanimity. As we have seen, Kolbe grew up on the Buchtel campus and was well-known on campus and in the community. He was generally respected, although Charles R. Olin, longtime business manager of the College, observed that he was "not a church man."

Kolbe started his administration with a flourish, announcing that $100,000 had been raised and another $100,000 pledged toward a $500,000 endowment, the figure required for Buchtel to become fully accredited by the new North Central Association of Colleges and Universities. At the same time, however, Kolbe announced that financial stringencies required an enrollment limit of 200 new students for the fall term of 1913. He called on the city of Akron to "give from her prosperity" to aid the College in its growth.

Commenting on Kolbe's statement, the *Akron Beacon Journal* noted that Akron had enough wealthy people to put up the remaining $300,000. Though this was undoubtedly true, the timing proved to be poor. In February 1913 came the first great strike in Akron's rubber industry. Waves of red-ribboned strikers surged through the streets, encouraged and inflamed by the rhetoric of Big Bill Haywood of the radical Industrial Workers of the World. Mayor Frank Rockwell ordered saloons to close; anti-strike citizens formed the Citizens Welfare League, donned yellow armbands, and countermarched in downtown streets. By the end of March the strike was over, but the strain of the past seven weeks had taken its toll of local optimism.

To compound the city's problem, torrential rains in March inundated parts of the city, flooding and even smashing many homes and commercial buildings. The twin blows of strike and flood ruined any hope that local sources might soon provide the additional $300,000 essential to continuing the College's work.

This was for Buchtel College "one of the most critical hours in her entire history." President Kolbe, despairing of raising private money, now set out to persuade Akron that the College served the city's residents more than any other group. He reminded citizens that the Universalist connection had been cut six years earlier; by 1913 only 16 of the 180 collegiate students were from Universalist families. The overwhelming majority of both collegiate and prep students lived in Akron and Summit County.

Kolbe had been impressed by a story in the *Cleveland Plain Dealer* about the municipal universities of Cincinnati and Toledo, and saw plainly that a university of this type would both serve Akron and answer the needs of Buchtel. At the April 14 Board meeting, he submitted a proposal that Buchtel College, including all physical properties and endowment, be offered to the City of Akron to be operated as a municipal university. The Board voted unanimously to make this proposition to the city through the Akron Charter Commission, then drafting a proposed city charter. The commission responded positively, appointed a committee to investigate the College's offer, and then sought information about the services that a municipal university could perform for the city.

To this end the commission consulted President C. F. Dabney of the University of Cincinnati. He emphasized that students at a municipal university, by living at home, could afford an education otherwise beyond their means, and that such a university could also provide training in the specialized services increasingly demanded by industry and business. Reassured by Dabney's confidence, the commission was convinced of the desirability and financial feasibility of the move. But fearing that the Buchtel College issue might jeopardize the charter's chances at the polls, they passed the Buchtel offer to the Akron City Council with a recommendation that it be placed separately on the ballot for a vote by the electorate.

For the next several months College officials waged an intense campaign to inform Akron voters of the advantages that a municipal university held for them. The *Beacon Journal* gave extensive coverage. The University, it said, would provide "free higher education to Akron's sons and daughters—rich or poor," and do so at "small cost to the taxpayer." A municipal university would attract a "desirable class of citizens" to Akron; suburban communities would be more willing to annex themselves to Akron so as to benefit from free tuition; free practical and technical training would stimulate Akron business and industry. The University could perform diverse specialized services for the city, from training teachers to performing chemical and engineering tests, giving psychological tests to school children, collecting historical information, and supervising civil service examinations.

The campaign had a positive effect. Pockets of misunderstanding and potential resistance to Buchtel's offer disappeared as popular appreciation of the advantages, coupled with the limited cost to the taxpayer, became clear. On July 28, the city council passed an ordinance providing for a special ballot at the September primary on the question "Shall Buchtel College be accepted by the City of Akron?" To the council's embarrassment, however, it discovered that an issue of this sort could be placed on the ballot only by initiative petition, a time-consuming process. Furthermore, the tax levy that would provide operating money for the university had to be enacted immediately if funds were to be collected in 1914. In response to these obstacles, the council decided to act on its own authority. The Buchtel Trustees formally offered the College to the Akron City Council on August 20. Five days later the council passed ordinance No. 4050 accepting the Trustees' offer "to transfer and convey the entire property, assets and endowments of [Buchtel] College to the City of Akron for a municipal university." Mayor Frank Rockwell signed the ordinance on August 26. It was accompanied by another ordinance that levied a half-mill tax in support of the municipal university. Both ordinances were to take effect September 24, 1913.

The Municipal University considered December 15, 1913, its true birthday, for on that day Mayor Rockwell appointed the new Board of Directors. The next day the Board met officially, named the school The Municipal University of Akron, and also named the arts and science college the Buchtel College of Liberal Arts, as required in the transfer agreement.

The new University fulfilled the promises made to the charter commission, the Akron City Council, and Akron voters. One promised service, a college of engineering, accepted its first students in September 1914. Dean Fred

Ayer brought with him from the University of Cincinnati the cooperative plan of engineering education, giving Akron an early foothold in that important educational movement. Engineering students soon were surveying city property and testing building and paving materials for the city. A Bureau of Industrial Research ran chemical analyses for smaller manufacturing concerns. The department of biology provided specialized public health training. The department of physical training helped supervise city playgrounds. Sociology students surveyed living conditions for wards of the courts. The political science department contributed materials toward a municipal research library. The Curtis School of Home Economics, established in 1914, became involved in a variety of community projects. The University also offered special evening courses to train scoutmasters, typists, social workers, YMCA workers, and teachers of "Americanism," whose main function was to prepare immigrants for naturalization. By the early 1920s, it had added commercial courses and a teacher training program, not to mention music lessons, dramatic productions, and public lectures.

The Municipal University soon required additional funds to meet its growing obligations and commitments, and the early 1920s were a poor time to seek such funds. Akron's frantic growth had continued through the World War I period until, in 1920, it was officially a city of 208,000. This frenetic growth put an intolerable burden on city resources. Tax monies were urgently needed for police and fire protection, education, recreation, sewers, and a host of other requirements of a growing city. Thus when Kolbe proposed additional tax revenue for the University, the suggestion was met with considerable hostility, especially from the *Beacon Journal,* which complained about "the high cost of professors."

And what of student reaction to the profound changes? Returning Buchtelites must have had a sharpened sense of anticipation as they arrived in September 1914 for their first full year in a municipal university. In the first issue of the student newspaper, the editor said what must have been in the minds of many:

It is with mingled emotions that Buchtel students regard this vital change in the control of their college. We who have spent a year or more at Buchtel cannot meditate over the matter without a feeling of regret that "Old Buchtel" is to lose something of her individuality as a privately endowed institution. Yet there can be no question that the students and faculty of Buchtel as a body are heartily in favor of the change, for they foresee in the not distant future a greater institution, a university of which we shall be proud to call ourselves alumni.

The great semicentennial celebration of 1920 marked the end of an era. Hundreds of Buchtel graduates mingled with the young University alumni. One of the original incorporators of Buchtel College, H. L. Canfield, then past 90 years of age, came from Los Angeles. Buchtel's second president, Everett L. Rexford, was on hand to greet his young successor and namesake, Parke Rexford Kolbe. The main address on this occasion was delivered by Samuel Capen, an educator who had first visited the campus in 1886 with his father, the president of Tufts. Capen emphasized "the complete change of structure and purpose" that the University had experienced. Thanks to this "almost providential . . . metamorphosis," the institution was now in "a position of exceptional strength" to meet the demands of a social order radically different from that of a generation earlier.

Four years later, Capen again visited Akron. He asked his audience:

> I wonder if you people of Akron realize exactly what has happened in the last ten years in the development of this institution? I think it is fair to say that no one would have expected that out of Buchtel College could have come in so short a time, an institution of such comprehensiveness, of such direct public service; an institution that perhaps more than any other represents our idea of the function of a municipal university.

And so Old Buchtel, a "country college" which had served so well the needs of its time and place, lived on in its worthy successor, The Municipal University of Akron.

12

Those Good Old College Days

he Buchtel College fire of 1899 marked a transition in many aspects of college life. Old customs vanished, especially those associated with dormitory life, and new ones took their place only to give way in turn to the still newer traditions of the Municipal University.

Hazing was among the first casualties. Though officially abolished in the 1890s, it had continued surreptitiously. It was closely associated with two customs enforced by the upper classes: that freshmen wear beanies and that they not appear in their class colors. Any violation brought swift reprisal. In October 1903, for example, when freshmen appeared at morning chapel exercises wearing their class colors, the *Buchtelite* called their action the equivalent of "placing a chip on the shoulder and daring a man to knock it off." President Church, anticipating trouble, told the upperclassmen that the faculty considered the freshmen duly initiated, but a brawl ensued anyway and the freshmen lost their colors. The faculty then suspended virtually the entire male student body, but this proved so obviously impractical that eleven upperclassmen were singled out for punishment. While their fate was being decided, the students amused themselves by marching around Buchtel Hall singing College songs. A compromise was reached: the custom was retained, but henceforth only sophomores could challenge freshmen, and since freshmen usually outnumbered sophomores, they generally held their own in subsequent confrontations. "Beanies" and hazing did not long survive the transition to the Municipal University.

Another tradition that failed to survive changing times was the annual "cremation" of selected textbooks on the Class Stone of '79 by black-robed graduating seniors. The class stones of '79 and '80 themselves retained their importance as focuses of student activity. The most recent tradition, beginning in the post–World War II era, is for student organizations to paint the stones with their group insignia.

Torchlight parades, bonfires, and spontaneous parades through downtown Akron are now but dim memories. Yet these were exciting and inexpensive ways for Buchtel students to celebrate—not always inexpensive, for on a few occasions students had to pay replacement costs for neighborhood fences and wooden sidewalks requisitioned as fuel. Among the most enthusiastic of the spontaneous student demonstrations was one celebrating the news that Robert Tucker, Class of '91, had won the state oratorical contest. Old Buchtel's dormitories rang with the College yell, the College bell pealed, a bonfire was set ablaze, and "an immense crowd of boys" paraded through downtown Akron, "making the night hideous" with horns and drums before returning to campus and firing a salute (with what, we are not told).

Among the traditions that *did* survive the private college

was the requirement that male students and faculty use the east stairs of the new Buchtel Hall, and female students and faculty the west stairs. Tradition in this case was bolstered by functional considerations, the men's restroom being by the east stairs and the women's by the west stairs. When the interior of Buchtel Hall was remodeled after being gutted by the 1971 fire, this tradition disappeared.

Another carryover from Buchtel College days is The University of Akron's Alma Mater. President A. B. Church wrote the lyrics to the Buchtel Alma Mater. School officials after 1913 simply substituted the name Akron for Buchtel, maintaining the meter exactly. Because the melody was that of the Cornell Hymn, which was used for the same purpose by innumerable high schools and colleges across the land, some people felt the Akron Alma Mater lacked distinction. In the 1950s an effort to replace it with Parke Kolbe's *Men of Akron* failed. In 1969 the committee organizing the 1970 centennial celebration invited proposals from anyone wishing to submit words and/or music for a new alma mater, but none of the entries was deemed an improvement. Indeed, the overwhelming sentiment was "Leave the Alma Mater alone, don't mess around with it!" Today, played by the Blue and Gold Marching Band in a striking arrangement introduced by Richard Jackoboice, it sounds as good as ever. The blue and gold colors are yet another carryover; these were the colors of Buchtel College.

As enrollment grew and the Municipal University fielded better athletic teams, students demanded a mascot, or a nickname, or both. They got the nickname, but not the mascot. Student Margaret Hamlin won a 1927 contest with her suggestion of "Zippers," a popular new brand of overshoes marketed by the B. F. Goodrich Company, which allowed the University to use the name. Some students complained that "Zippers" was not a name to inspire heroic deeds, but in its later contraction—"Zips"—it was unique, recognizable, and readily adaptable to newsmen's needs. It fit headlines, banners, and announcements; it also lent itself to cheers and to the lyrics of *The Akron Blue and Gold*, Akron's fight song, written by Fred Waring and first played on his weekly radio program in 1939.

Early in the 1950s student leaders chose the kangaroo as a mascot, but this creature seemed too remote from any Akron connection to catch on. Sentiment changed, however, with the appearance of "Zippy" in 1954. This human kangaroo has charmed Zip fans to such an extent that no athletic event is complete without him (or her?). The robust marsupial with the friendly smile also visits children in hospitals, charms local gatherings, and spreads goodwill for the University.

Many University traditions center around athletic contests. Buchtel College customarily played Case, Wooster, Kenyon, Hiram, Mount Union, and other small colleges. The Municipal University continued these rivalries through affiliation with the Ohio Athletic Conference. A keen new competition with neighboring Kent State University emerged in the 1930s and grew into Akron's principal rivalry in the post–World War II years. By the 1970s, it had grown so intense and pre-game student pranks had become so destructive that officials of both schools tried to cool it down; but it remained a great rivalry even as Akron moved up in athletic competition from the NCAA's Division II, to Division 1-AA, and finally to Division 1-A, the top of the heap. Along the way intense competition developed with

Youngstown, Eastern Kentucky, and Middle Tennessee. By the end of the 1980s, Akron was trying to adjust to new conference alignments that promised more enduring rivalries.

Nothing, however, matched the enthusiasm generated by the annual Acme-Zip extravaganza held each September at the Rubber Bowl. This successful promotion was inaugurated in 1954 when Athletic Director Kenneth "Red" Cochrane, President Norman P. Auburn, and key officials from the F. W. Albrecht Grocery Company and the *Akron Beacon Journal* developed an extended program of football games, soccer matches, and other colorful events that packed in the spectators. More than a University event, it was a community extravaganza.

Football and bands go together. Buchtel College had small musical groups of instrumentalists at athletic contests; today we would call such a group a "pep" band. During Municipal University days it was difficult to field a marching band since a disproportionate number of students worked off campus and could not afford the time to practice. Nevertheless, Darrel "Red" Witters, instrumental music director in the 1940s and 1950s, assembled peppy, enthusiastic bands that featured the Zippettes and the inimitable rolling bass drum. This instrument, a bass drum mounted within a huge tire that rolled along while the drummer walked alongside beating it, was a national "first." Led by the irrepressible Witters, band members enlivened many campus gatherings, playing Christmas carols in the student center, performing at student assemblies, and generally contributing to good spirits on campus. Today's marching band, "Ohio's Pride," is highly disciplined and professionally polished. Like its predecessors, it contributes to the excitement and enthusiasm of campus events and represents the University in the community.

Among the new Municipal University traditions was Engineer's Day, which emerged in the 1920s as a St. Patrick's Day celebration. A favorite part of the day for many students and for some faculty came in the morning when St. Pat, the "original rivet slinger," would rise from his coffin and lead a noisy, motley throng of engineering students through University buildings emptying classrooms of their "captives." Other activities involved repelling liberal arts students intent on capturing the engineer's flag, painting dogs or an occasional freshman, lifting coed skirts with an air jet installed in a busy doorway, and various contests like beard growing and tobacco spitting. The evening was capped by the Engineer's Brawl at some local retreat. Like the publication "Engin-Ears," banned by President Hezzleton Simmons for its "ribald humor," Engineer's Day, too, passed into history as a result of administrative action in the early 1960s.

Other University traditions evolved around the ROTC. First established nationally in 1919 by a committee of educators that included Akron's President Kolbe, the Reserve Officers Training Corps flourished on the Akron campus. All freshmen and sophomore men were required to participate. Its two honorary societies, Scabbard and Blade and Pershing Rifles, sponsored various activities, and the annual military review held for visiting inspecting officers was colorful. The ROTC-sponsored Military Ball brought outstanding dance bands to Akron for one of the premier social gatherings of the season. These events vanished in the 1960s and 1970s as the ROTC program temporarily fell out of favor. Despite a resurgence of interest,

ROTC no longer plays the visible role on campus that it did in the past.

Another University tradition, Homecoming, had roots in the early days of Buchtel College, when it was associated with June commencement ceremonies and class reunions. It later became an annual fall celebration centered around a football game, a Homecoming Dance, and the crowning of a Homecoming Queen. Following World War II the parade featured spectacular floats. Spicer School children crowded the parade route, and University students lined Buchtel Avenue as the floats made their way to downtown Akron, then past Children's Hospital, and finally to the grounds of Stan Hywet, Akron's great historic mansion, where they remained on display. Recent Homecoming celebrations remain lively, with action centered on the football game and on Jackson Field activities.

Founder's Day was first observed in 1882 when Buchtel students and faculty sought to honor John R. Buchtel and others who had contributed to the school's founding. Though observed annually since then, it has been held at various times during the school year and has taken many forms. The wreath ceremony remains a standard part of the celebration. Wreaths from the convocation site are taken by student leaders to the Glendale Cemetery graves of John and Elizabeth Buchtel and Parke and Lydia Kolbe, the Kolbes being honored for their part in founding the Municipal University. Recently Founder's Day has become incorporated into the celebration of May Day.

May Day, another all-campus event that has evolved through the years, started in the administration of President Church as Tree Day. It became the principal springtime festival, complete with an elaborate crowning of a

May Queen and a formal dance. Since classes were dismissed at noon, students would have deemed it a success even without the ceremonies. In recent years queen crownings and dances have given way to more informal activities on Jackson Field and the Buchtel Common.

Commencement is perhaps the most traditional of all academic events. In Buchtel College's early years the ceremonies lasted for the better part of three days and included elaborate class reunions. It took the patience of a saint to sit through commencement exercises, with speeches, orations, musical selections, and prayers stretching on *ad infinitum*. Although Buchtel College could accommodate the graduates and friends of the College in the chapel, the modern University has never had adequate space on campus for commencement ceremonies, which have been held in the Central High School auditorium, the Akron Armory, the Blossom Music Center, and the Coliseum. The first was quickly outgrown; the other three were less than ideal. By the time the E. J. Thomas Performing Arts Hall became available, graduating classes were too large for the facility. By the 1980s they were too large for the James A. Rhodes Arena. Among recent expedients have been a midyear commencement, two ceremonies on the same day (with the graduating class being split by colleges), and a separate ceremony for the School of Law. Virtually the only untried locale is the Rubber Bowl, and given the chanciness of weather, that is probably a good thing.

Although the University can no longer be viewed as an extended family, campus traditions remain important. They serve to help faculty, students, and alumni see themselves as an institution that has stood the test of time.

13

Fraternities, Sororities, and Honoraries

ong after formal courses have become but a dim memory, college graduates tend to remember the friendships and associations they made in campus activities, in social groups, and in college hangouts. Probably the most intensive alumni loyalties are generated by fraternities and sororities, which provide a continuing role for alums in the activities of the local chapter.

Buchtel College and The University of Akron compiled a remarkable record of fraternity and sorority participation, even though Buchtel College had few students who could readily afford the costs and Akron, during its municipal phase, had no dormitories. Many students, moreover, worked and had little time or money for social activities. Yet within these limits, the Hilltop campus managed to sustain a vital fraternity and sorority system.

The Greek system in American colleges was in its early stages of expansion when Buchtel men and women became involved. In 1873 Delta Tau Delta established its Eta chapter at Buchtel. It was the fifth chapter of that fraternity, started fourteen years earlier at Bethany College. In 1875 nine Buchtel men were initiated into the Ohio Eta chapter of Phi Delta Theta, one of the "Miami Triad." Both fraternities fitted out rented rooms in Akron's business district.

On Founder's Day of 1882 eight men joined to form the Lone Star fraternity (Pi Kappa Epsilon). It quickly adopted all the characteristics of the other groups, including a suite of rooms off campus. Tradition holds that Lone Star is the oldest surviving local fraternity in America.

Buchtel's three fraternities flourished until the severe depression of 1893–97, when the number of men enrolled in collegiate courses declined dramatically. Delta Tau Delta was so depleted that it surrendered its charter to the national office in 1895, an especially galling move because one of its own, Frank Wieland, Class of '90, later became president of the national group. Seventy-seven years later Delta Tau Delta would be reactivated on the Akron campus. Phi Delta Theta had a similar experience, surrendering its charter in 1896. For many years thereafter the Phi Delts maintained a local fraternity, until ultimately the national rechartered the local group as its Ohio Epsilon chapter. Lone Star, inactive during 1896–97, was reinvigorated by a group of students who incorporated it under the laws of Ohio in 1898.

Sororities were also established during Buchtel's first decade. Three women joined to form the Lambda chapter of Kappa Kappa Gamma in 1877. They met secretly in their dormitory rooms until the authorities recognized them and assigned them more spacious quarters in West Hall. In 1886 Lambda chapter entertained the national Kappa convention, using the Phi Delta Theta rooms for the occasion.

Tragedy struck the Kappas in 1890 in their West Hall room. While the young women in festive attire were holding a social, one member brushed her hat against an open gas mantle. The hat ignited, and flames spread to her gauze dress. The flames spread instantly to those attempting to beat out the conflagration. Two members died that night, and a third perished later from burns. Six other young women were seriously burned but survived.

Buchtel's second nineteenth-century sorority, Eta chapter of Delta Gamma, was chartered in 1879. The DGs also met in dormitory rooms. They sent one of the two delegations that made up the first national Delta Gamma convention in Oxford, Mississippi, in 1881. Two years later Buchtel hosted the national convention; the attendance could not have been large, for the banquet was held at the Akron residence of Jessie Tibbals. In 1893 the national again met in Akron, this time at the Universalist church. The local chapter also initiated and directed publication of the sorority's journal, *The Anchora*. Today Eta chapter remains the oldest continuously functioning of Delta Gamma's approximately 200 chapters.

Only one other sorority was chartered at Buchtel College. Phi Mu, started in 1907 as a local, received its national charter in 1912, the sorority's first chapter north of the Mason-Dixon line. Phi Mu also became the first Akron sorority to occupy its own full-sized quarters when, in 1927, it acquired a house on Buchtel Avenue near the campus.

These early Greek organizations competed with one another in every aspect of college life. The rushing of new members was unrestricted, leading to various excesses. The social snobbery long associated with these closed societies and that perennial campus conflict—the "ins" versus the "outs"—left unaffiliated students with negative atti-

tudes. From time to time the faculty talked about the need to restrain the chapters, but little seems to have been done. No matter how competitive they were among themselves, the Greeks banded together to defend the fraternity and sorority system when threatened with outside interference.

Fraternities and sororities had an image problem in the Municipal University's early years. It became particularly acute in 1914–15, when stress between Greeks and non-Greeks threatened to embarrass the University. The details are no longer clear, but the University's Board of Directors informed the faculty that it "viewed with rising alarm" the internal dissension among the fraternities "as reported by current talk among our citizens and even by articles in the local papers." The Directors called for a careful examination of fraternities, their influence on student life, and especially their alleged "detrimental influence upon the activities of the whole student body." The faculty was requested to investigate and report; it did so as the crisis passed, and the fraternities became more circumspect.

World War I put a damper on fraternity activity as men became scarce on campus. Following the war, fraternities and sororities came under increased control from the University administration, especially from Dean of Men Donfred H. Gardner, but both maintained their vigor through the throes of the Great Depression of the 1930s. As World War II drained manpower from the campus, fraternity life declined; but its decline was offset by a flourishing sorority life on the predominantly female campus. When former servicemen flooded back in the postwar years, fraternities again prospered. Although most veterans were in a rush to complete their college education, many were also eager for social contacts. As one might expect, they had no patience with the hazing and pranks associated with initiation. A man who had recently been in mortal combat was not about to allow some eighteen-year-old to paddle him.

In the 1920s and 1930s the charters of most Greek organizations had exclusionary clauses that limited membership on the basis of race, religion, and ethnicity. They were unashamedly WASP societies. New fraternity and sorority chapters emerged to accommodate students left out of the system. Theta Phi Alpha pledged Catholic women, Alpha Epsilon Pi pledged Jewish men, and Delta Pi Iota pledged Jewish women. By the 1950s nationals were repudiating exclusionary rules, and the new chapters, their work done, disappeared from campus.

Although fraternities and sororities also eliminated racial restrictions from their charters, black students felt a need for their own organizations. In 1957–58 the Sphinx Club received a charter as the Alpha Tau chapter of a black fraternity, Alpha Phi Alpha. Thanks in part to its national affiliation and the energetic leadership of its alumni, this fraternity became a considerable force in community affairs, especially by its efforts in building and managing major housing developments. In like manner the Ivyettes, a local for black women, received a charter in 1961–62 from Alpha Kappa Alpha sorority. They, too, were involved in community action programs.

Other accomplishments can be credited to Akron's fraternities and sororities during the productive years from 1945 to 1965. Several Akron locals won their national's outstanding chapter award. The Phi Delta Theta chorus played a visible role at the fraternity's national conventions. In 1953–54 Akron's fraternities had the highest fraternity grade point average in the nation, and fraternity and sorority grade point averages consistently exceeded the all-campus level. A promising development was the elimination of destructive hazing practices. "Hell Week" gave way to "Help Week," which substituted constructive community service for traditional shenanigans.

During this same period nonaffiliated students organized an Independent Student Organization, which took part in Stunt Night and other competitions traditionally associated with the fraternities and sororities. As a host of more specialized interest groups developed among unaffiliated students in the 1970s and 1980s, interest in the Independent Student Organization waned, and it disappeared from campus.

Interest in the fraternities and sororities also waned dur-

ing the late 1960s and early 1970s, a period of student
protest against everything that appeared to be part of the
so-called "establishment." Antiwar protests, black civil
rights agitation, and feminist assertiveness contributed to
student challenges directed at the administration, the curriculum, and student organizations. The initiative seemed
to be with the protestors, whether they were picketing
corporate recruiters, occupying Buchtel Hall, or holding
"free University" sessions under improvised conditions.
To many of them fraternity and sorority life seemed some-
how immoral or beside the point.

Still, the Greek organizations survived, and slowly re-
vived as the protest era died. By the early 1980s a reinvigorated fraternity and sorority system was much in evidence. One sign of its renewed vigor was the appearance
of new and improved housing for the various chapters.
Continuous expansion of the campus had forced many
groups to relocate, several of them more than once. The
Lone Star property on Fir Hill, for example, was torn down
to make way for the Olin Hall parking lot. After occupying
the former Florence Crittenton Home property on Buchtel
Avenue for some years, the Lone Stars finally acquired a
new home in the area lying between Spicer Street and the
Akron Expressway, where many other Greek groups were
located. Others such as Phi Kappa Tau and Delta Gamma
built houses on campus, some soon to be nearly encircled
by parking lots. The University assisted some groups by
renting dormitory space in the larger houses, but an old
dream of a fraternity and sorority row, financed by the
University, failed to materialize.

From an early time Greek letters denoted not only fraternities and sororities, but also honorary societies. Among the oldest of these still active is Phi Sigma Alpha, established by the Class of '10 to recognize scholarship. Today it is the scholastic honor society for the Buchtel College of Arts and Sciences, performing the function that Phi Beta Kappa performs nationally. Among others that date back to the Municipal University are Sigma Tau (1924) in engineering and Kappa Delta Pi (1925) in education. Many departmental honoraries also existed by the 1920s, including some that later disappeared. In the 1960s, when University officials approached the national office of Pi Gamma Nu, a social sciences honorary, to inquire about establishing a chapter on the Hilltop, they were informed to their embarrassment that Akron had been a charter member of the national 40 years earlier.

Activities honoraries have also played an important campus role. The national men's leadership honorary, Omicron Delta Kappa (ODK), established Theta Circle in 1922. Today it is the eighth oldest chapter of a national that boasts more than 200 chapters. ODK's counterpart among women, a local named Pierian, in 1964 became a chapter of Mortar Board, the national women's activities honorary. In recent years, both ODK and Mortar Board removed gender limitations, with the result that many men and women are members of both.

Although it is not a society, one other activities honor award should be mentioned. In the early 1920s, the faculty devised a twelve-point rating scale for selecting students worthy of receiving an "Akron Honor Key." Over the years the qualifications have changed, but the award of an "A-Key" is still a coveted student honor.

14

"We Are State!"

Few persons arriving at The University of Akron or the first time have any idea of the number of organizational changes it has gone through since its founding. Although it is not uncommon for colleges and universities to evolve through various administrative structures, few have operated under as many different organizational forms as Akron.

Buchtel College was a private, church-related liberal arts college until 1907, when it severed its connection to the Ohio Universalist Convention. It remained a private college for six more years until becoming The Municipal University of Akron. It became a state-assisted municipal university in 1963, and four years later took its place as a full-fledged state university. It is time now to look briefly at its transition to state status.

Early in the 1960s, as Akron was assuming a place among the best of the nation's municipal schools, University officials increasingly realized that municipal universities had a limited future. This recognition had nothing to do with the quality of the education they provided; it was largely a matter of money.

The Akron metropolitan area was growing rapidly in the 1950s and 1960s, but that growth was primarily outside Akron's corporate limits. The city's tax contribution was not increasing fast enough to provide the new revenue needed by the rapidly expanding and improving university, and political observers were skeptical about Akron citizens' readiness to accept tax increases for this purpose. Since student enrollment growth promised to continue, new sources of revenue were essential. The best hope was the state of Ohio.

Ohio's municipal universities—Akron, Cincinnati, and Toledo—had first sought state aid in the 1920s. They had renewed their effort in the 1950s but failed to win the support of Governor Michael DiSalle or the state legislature.

The situation brightened in 1963 when James A. Rhodes became governor. Rhodes agreed with President Norman Auburn that a state subvention to cover part of the costs of freshmen and sophomores would be the most economical way for the state to expand public higher education. Rhodes told Akronites that they were being "double taxed" because they paid the same taxes that other Ohioans paid to support the state universities, and then paid additional taxes to support the municipal university. He promptly endorsed a bill calling for a state subvention for every full-time freshman and sophomore in the municipal university. The general assembly passed the bill, and Governor Rhodes signed it into law on July 1, 1963.

This new source of income, helpful as it was, provided only eight to eleven percent of the University's annual operating income, and the ink was scarcely dry on the new law before University leaders were sounding out the pros-

pects for greater involvement in the state system. Key legislators, the governor, and above all the new Board of
Regents were approached. The Regents were critically important, since Akron, as a state-assisted university, was
fully bound by their policies.

Dr. Harold Oyster, the able and knowledgeable first
Chairman of the Board of Regents, was a veteran of Republican politics in Ohio and of the general assembly. It
was a real coup, therefore, when Auburn persuaded him
to accept a position as Vice-President for Development on
the Hilltop campus. With his Columbus connections, Oyster was instrumental in helping Akron move toward full
state university status. Auburn and Chairman of the Board
Harry Schrank handled the behind-the-scenes chores and
plans that forwarded the cause.

The Board of Regents, meanwhile, hired the Academy
for Educational Development to study state-financed higher
education, and its report—*The Master Plan for State Policy
in Higher Education*—convincingly demonstrated the need,
especially in northeastern Ohio, for additional state-sup-
ported higher education. Among other recommendations,
it urged that Akron be made a full-fledged member of the
state system.

To accomplish this end, Oyster and Dean Stanley Samad
of the School of Law drafted an enabling bill that was
introduced in the legislature by state senators Oliver Ocasek (D), a professor in the college of education, and Edward Garrigan (R), an Akron alumnus. Three groups
opposed the bill. Some Democratic members of the legislature felt that additional state universities would mean
additional taxes, for which they were reluctant to vote.
Existing state universities had related misgivings: they

claimed with some justice that the tax pie was already too small and should not be cut into more pieces. Finally, some Akron alumni and local boosters in the city worried that the University would lose its historic character, and in particular that Akron students would lose their preference in admission and be displaced by students from outside the city. To this last group University officials responded with assurances that no qualified Akron student would be turned away, that the University still regarded Akron as the focus of its service, and that the name—The University of Akron—would endure.

Years of planning and effort came to a successful end on July 29, 1965, when the Ohio General Assembly passed amended Senate Bill 212. On December 5, the Board of Directors unanimously agreed to convert The University of Akron to a state university. President Auburn likened their decision to that made by the Trustees of Buchtel College in 1913, when they changed the character of the institution rather than let it languish or die of financial malnutrition. The change from municipal to state status would be far less drastic, since Akron had been an open-admission public university since 1951. State university status would not change the type of students enrolled except, by eliminating the resident fee advantage formerly enjoyed by Akronites, to attract more students from outside Akron's city limits.

Four steps were now required to complete the transition. First, the University's Directors agreed to transfer the assets, property, and obligations of the Board to a new Board of Trustees. Second, the Akron City Council unanimously adopted an ordinance to submit the conversion to the Akron electorate. Third, President Auburn and Chair-

man Schrank, representing the University, and Chancellor John Millet, representing the Board of Regents, signed the necessary agreements with Governor Rhodes as witness.

The fourth step was completed successfully on May 3, 1966, when Akron voters overwhelmingly approved the conversion proposal by a nine-to-one margin. They also approved overwhelmingly—35,142 to 4,665—the accompanying measure whereby city taxes to support the Municipal University were to terminate at the end of 1967. Election officials thought this to be the most conclusive vote ever recorded on a Summit County issue. "No one," said the *Akron Beacon Journal*, "could have been surprised that Akron voters overwhelmingly approved the two issues," since the benefits were obvious for all to see. It was clear, said the writer, that "the physical properties . . . the student body, the faculty, and, most important, the intangible spirit which is the heart of the university will remain unmoved and unchanged."

Late in the spring of 1967, the state legislature approved operating funds for the University and the new Board of Trustees assumed its duties. Students expressed their satisfaction in a *Buchtelite* headline: "We Are State!"

15

Plato to Polymers
The Curriculum

he heart of every college and university is its curriculum, that complex of courses and degree options that make up the instructional program. Students now entering The University of Akron are sometimes overwhelmed by the great variety of degree programs and career choices available to them. That was not true of Buchtel College students, whose options were severely limited.

The core of Buchtel's collegiate program was the four-year Classical Course, which led to the Bachelor of Arts degree. Only applicants with a strong three-year secondary school background could meet this program's admission standards. Students were required to have some facility in Latin and Greek grammar, to be familiar with the writings of Xenophon, Homer, Caesar, Virgil, and Cicero, and to have a solid background in algebra, English grammar, United States history, and ancient and modern geography. Except for a lighter emphasis on mathematics, these admission standards were essentially those of Yale and the other recognized centers of excellence against which Buchtel measured itself.

Once embarked on the Classical Course, the young scholar could look forward to two years of intensive work in Latin and Greek, and to additional courses in French, German, and English, including rhetoric, themes, declamations, oral and written reviews, and "voice culture." Also to be mastered were mathematics through calculus, physiology, zoology, botany, geology, mineralogy, field surveying, chemistry, natural philosophy, intellectual philosophy, logic, "moral science," Greek and Roman history, English literature, political economy, mechanics, astronomy, and Guizot's *History of Civilization*. As long as Buchtel endured, this curriculum was essentially unchanged, although after 1882 the elective system gave it modest flexibility. Only a small number of the collegiate students enrolled in this demanding course.

For the less well-prepared—or the less solvent or ambitious—a two-year Philosophical Course was offered: a shortened version of the Classical Course that did not require Latin and Greek. It was lengthened twice in the 1870s, emerging as a full four-year course leading to the Bachelor of Philosophy degree.

A Scientific Course became a four-year program in 1875. It focused on the natural and physical sciences and led to the Bachelor of Science degree, which was viewed somewhat patronizingly by those who were or sought to become Bachelors of Arts. Each collegiate course had a corresponding preparatory course.

Students who wished to teach in elementary or secondary school could meet state requirements by taking a two-year Normal Course offered in the preparatory department.

Other students' preparation did not fit any prescribed course of study. They were classified as "irregular," their programs were individually tailored, and they were awarded a "certificate of completion."

Learning resources available to students and faculty were severely limited in Buchtel's early years. Since there were no scientific laboratories in the original college structure, professors had to improvise. Professor Charles Knight enlisted student labor to create a primitive chemistry lab in the basement of Old Buchtel. Professor Edward Claypole taught geology and natural sciences with minimal equipment. He was inventive, however, taking his classes on field trips to the Cuyahoga Gorge and the Portage Lakes. His great contribution as a teacher was to have each of his students undertake a thorough investigation of a specialized subject, to give them some idea of the charm and discipline of research. He showed them how to fashion their own primitive lab equipment from tin cans and other ordinary objects.

The College treasured collections of fossils, minerals, and natural history specimens donated by faculty and friends, including President McCollester himself. Used for study, these collections also had public relations value: impressive pictures of them graced the catalog and permitted the College to brag about its superior instruction in the sciences. These irreplaceable collections were totally destroyed in the 1899 fire.

In earlier pages we described the first library and its restricted use. Its presence, too, allowed the College to boast, even though few students had access to the locked cases in which the books were displayed. We have also noted the work of Professor Charles S. Howe in erecting an astronomical observatory on campus. This teaching tool appears to have been little used after his departure from the faculty.

College curricula are always under tension from conflicting interests. By its very nature a college or university must preserve and transmit society's cultural heritage while pursuing new lines of intellectual inquiry. Disciplines that focus on the traditional are often in tension with those that change with great rapidity, whether the changes arise from new advances in knowledge or are based on little more than a reclassifying of subject matter. The pressure to include new or different subjects in the college curriculum goes well back into the nineteenth century; it was very much in evidence almost from Buchtel's beginnings.

A curricular evolution started quietly in American colleges during the 1870s and 1880s when President Charles Eliot of Harvard popularized the elective system, forcing every college to consider its own courses of study in relation to the new thrust. As Frederick Rudolph wrote in his history of American colleges, the "intellectual anarchy" of the elective system, coupled with a rising secularism, often meant "a loss of old purpose without the discovery of new purpose."

In 1882 Buchtel College adopted the elective system. Judging from Harvard's timetable, Buchtel was among the first colleges to get on the bandwagon, and once aboard it embraced the system with enthusiasm. With new options now established, there was a predictable push to introduce new courses to the curriculum. By the 1890s, for example, photography, still more a technique than an art form, was being taught. In 1895 Buchtel Trustee A. C.

Voris urged his colleagues to establish a school of manual training and industrial arts to serve industry's need for trained personnel. Judge Voris was confident the city of Akron would finance a chair, but the city was too poor to act at the time. His plan, in altered form, finally materialized in the 1960s when the Community and Technical College became an academic arm of The University of Akron.

Commercial courses and extension courses were first offered in President Church's administration, partly in response to local requests and partly in the hope that they would bring the College much-needed income. As we have seen, the transfer of Buchtel's assets to the city of Akron was rationalized in part by assuring citizens and Akron City Council members that a municipally financed university could support an expanded curriculum that would include courses beneficial to the community's need. And so it proved.

The Municipal University of Akron was but nine months old when the college of engineering opened to students. Coincidentally, the Curtis School of Home Economics was established under the direction of Professor Sarah Stimmel. As World War I stimulated the city's economy, Akron's burgeoning industries and service businesses demanded trained personnel, and the University responded with commercial courses and the beginnings of a secretarial science program. Dean Fred Ayer, who brought the cooperative program to the college of engineering, was also responsible for the commercial curriculum. Believing that he should have practical experience in this field, he secured a part-time job selling bathrobes at O'Neil's department store; students happily dubbed him "the bathrobe king." But Ayer was convinced of the co-op system's value and made it part of the course requirements in commerce. Even young women were sent out on co-op jobs, presumably a first in the nation.

This period saw an increase in the number of separate departments of instruction—chemistry, biology, physical training, history, modern languages, and others—and the creation of a teacher's college, the University's first step in expanding and professionalizing teacher training. Next, in a joint venture with the Akron Board of Education, the University took over direction of Perkins Normal Institute in Akron, and enrollments soared under a program described by some enthusiasts as the "best in the state." In the 1930s ties with the Akron Board of Education were severed, and the newly named College of Education was henceforth strictly a University operation.

As the University moved toward more specialized and practical curricula, it was in step with American higher education generally. Behind the scenes, however, smoldered an intensifying debate over the objectives of a college education. In its simplest form, the question is this: Do we educate students to make a life, or to make a living? Yet few traditionalists were so adamant as to suggest retaining the old classical curriculum in its entirety, and few of the "modernists" were so rash as to suggest casting it out entirely.

In the mid-1930s The University of Akron worked out an acceptable compromise. Along with Columbia, the University of Chicago, the University of Minnesota, and a few other American universities, it was in the vanguard of the General Education movement. In 1934 the University Council (composed of faculty and administrators) accepted three objectives for an undergraduate education. Students were to take courses surveying the chief fields of knowledge, they were to develop a sense of social responsibility, and they were to prepare for greater social and individual effectiveness in public service, in commerce and industry, and in the professions. To achieve these goals all students in the "lower" college (the freshman and sophomore years) would take a year each of English, Introduction to the Social Sciences, Introduction to the Natural Sciences, and Introduction to the Humanities. They were also to take physical education and a course in physical and mental hygiene, a year's work in either mathematics, accounting, or a foreign language, and the introductory courses in their major field. After completing the first two years with at least a 2.0 grade point average, they would be promoted to one of the "upper," degree-granting colleges, where specialized courses in one's major discipline were emphasized. To implement this plan, all academic advising for freshmen and sophomores was delegated to the dean of students and his advising staff. They sought to know the "whole student," dealing with academic and personal problems within the same advising context.

This pattern, with modest adjustments, endured through the unsettled period of economic depression, World War II, and the early postwar years. The survey courses became identified in student minds with their principal lecturers—Roy Sherman in the social sciences, Paul Acquarone in the natural sciences, and Don Keister in the humanities. Since every student was exposed to these courses, all could appreciate the many stories that circulated about the three lecturers.

By 1955 it was clearly time to revise the program. It was

now called the General Studies program, and although it retained broad survey courses, the overall requirements were modified in response to academic pressures. Options were made available. One could bypass the new course in Reasoning and Understanding Science by taking conventional introductory courses in the physical and natural sciences. In similar fashion one could bypass Institutions in the United States by taking appropriate courses in the social sciences. Western Cultural Traditions and a later course addition, Eastern Civilization, remained mandatory.

As in most academic endeavors, success depends less on the course material than on the quality of instruction. And so it was in the General Studies courses. It took an extraordinary lecturer—Thomas Sumner in Reasoning and Understanding Science, or David Riede in Western Cultural Traditions—to hold student interest. Not even superior instruction worked in every case. Sumner, for instance, spent several lectures developing the eighteenth-century Phlogiston Theory in order to illustrate how scientists reasoned, only to find that some students were not amused when he finally revealed that the theory was all wrong. "Forget the funny stuff; what's the right answer?" seemed to be their feeling.

Throughout the late 1960s and early 1970s, many of America's great universities succumbed to student pressure and scrapped survey courses and core curricula. In recent years most have scrambled to restore a core curriculum, realizing anew that common discourse among educated people is impossible unless they share a basic knowledge of our heritage and of our natural and physical environment. The University of Akron did not give in to the anarchistic sentiments of the time. The idea that breadth in the undergraduate curriculum was a necessary balance to depth in specialized fields was still viable on the Hilltop campus. The General Studies program survived intact, but it remained under continuing pressures for change as educational philosophies and practical interests competed for attention.

While general studies evolved in the 1950s and beyond, curricular expansion became endemic. President Norman P. Auburn had a clear vision of how the University might serve the public from which it drew its financial support, and, as enrollment exploded in the 1950s and 1960s, new degree-granting colleges emerged. The College of Business Administration led the way in 1953. In 1959 the proprietary Akron Law School became the University's College of Law (later School of Law).

In the 1960s Governor James A. Rhodes made strong efforts to persuade Ohio's public universities to offer vocationally oriented courses. Through its Associate Program, Akron already had experience in this field, and after careful study the Community and Technical College, granting associate degrees, was organized in 1964. The "experts" said it would never work to house technical programs on the same campus with baccalaureate degree programs. The experts were wrong, and the vigor of that college continues to contribute to the University's mission.

In 1967 the College of Nursing was organized, growing out of the limited nursing programs that had been offered for many years. That same year the departments of art, home economics, speech, and music were separated from the Buchtel College of Liberal Arts (later renamed Buchtel College of Arts and Sciences) to become the nucleus of the College of Fine and Applied Arts.

One goal that eluded the University, despite Auburn's persistent efforts, was a medical school. Having allotted a new college of medicine to the city of Toledo in 1964, the state legislature was reluctant to make another major investment in medical education. Not until the early 1970s were legislators persuaded that a medical school in northeastern Ohio could use existing hospital resources for clinical studies instead of constructing an expensive new teaching hospital. Other selling points were assurances that many doctors graduating from this institution would remain in the state and that many would be trained as family physicians, who were then in short supply. President Dominic J. Guzzetta played a key role in working out a cooperative arrangement with Kent State and Youngstown State universities whereby the three universities jointly sponsored the new Northeastern Ohio Universities College of Medicine. This arrangement has been a pacesetter nationally, demonstrating how high-quality medical education can be achieved at reasonable cost.

Still another new college emerged in 1988 when President William V. Muse, Dean Frank Kelley, and their staffs created the College of Polymer Science and Polymer Engineering, the first of its kind anywhere. Building on the University's most renowned professional program, the new college consolidated activities formerly carried on in a variety of academic units. It occupies the striking "polymer tower," an appropriate visual sign of the program's central role in the University and the community.

Along with increased speculation in the undergraduate

realm came the development of graduate programs. For several decades following 1914, when the faculty had first voted a residence requirement for a graduate degree, a few masters degrees were awarded, mostly in education. After World War II, growing professionalization in rubber chemistry and polymers provided the stimulus for the University's first doctoral program, which was fashioned in 1956 from what was clearly the University's most sophisticated research program. In succeeding years doctoral work expanded into other disciplines; by the late 1980s more than a dozen departments were awarding doctoral degrees.

While the curriculum was becoming more sophisticated, the University's evening courses kept pace. Evening classes designed to meet the needs of Akron's diverse student population were first offered on a regular basis in 1915. As a matter of University policy, virtually every degree program can be completed by taking only evening courses. It is doubtful that any university ever had a more complete commitment to evening work.

Ironically, the rush toward specialization tended to result in a new inflexibility reminiscent of the rigid curricula of a hundred years ago. In the graduate realm, courses in cognate fields partly offset the narrowness of masters and doctoral programs. In a number of undergraduate degree programs, however, only the General Studies requirement forced the student beyond the narrow bounds of the major discipline.

Although one might argue that in the modern world the specialist has prevailed over the generalist, curricula continue to evolve. And the Hilltop campus still seeks to maintain that community of discourse among educated persons that was central to Buchtel College.

16

Building for Tomorrow
A Modern Campus Emerges

s The University of Akron entered its 120th year, it occupied a campus more than thirty times the size of Old Buchtel during its heyday. The contemporary campus stretches from Main Street on the west to the Akron Expressway on the east; from the Ballet Center on the north to Buchtel Field and Folk Hall on the south. It completely encircles the tiny five-acre campus (exclusive of Buchtel Field) that had accommodated 198 collegiate students and about the same number of preps during Buchtel's last year as a private institution. The University has outgrown its hilltop.

And should anyone doubt that it was (and still is) a hilltop, try the following experiment. On a warm, muggy summer afternoon, walk briskly from the front of the Polsky building on Main Street to the front door of Buchtel Hall. The experience will provide a new perspective on the thinking of the Universalists and John R. Buchtel when they selected Spicer Hill Cemetery as their college site.

We left our account of early campus development in 1913, when President Parke R. Kolbe was looking forward optimistically to the construction of buildings to house new academic programs. Things went well at first. The college of engineering got a new laboratory building in 1916, and that same year a red-brick, Italianate structure named Carl F. Kolbe Hall was opened to house Bierce Library. Then came World War I, a postwar depression, and chaotic conditions in the city of Akron. All further construction stopped except for completion of a 5,000-seat concrete grandstand named Alumni Memorial Stadium at Buchtel Field.

When Kolbe left Akron in 1925, his successor, George F. Zook, took up the challenge of campus expansion. His only success was the Guggenheim Airship Institute, which was erected at the Akron Municipal Airport with money from the Guggenheim Foundation and a city bond issue. Research in lighter-than-air craft, directed in part by Cal Tech's world-renowned mathematician Theodore Von Karman, was conducted at the Institute, which boasted the world's largest vertical wind tunnel.

Zook devoted most of his energy to a controversial plan, inherited from Kolbe, to relocate the campus on 60 acres of open land just west of Hawkins Avenue on Akron's west side. There was considerable local opposition to a move that many misinterpreted as a desertion of Akron's most needy citizens for the benefit of a country club elite. As one old labor union battler said, the school helped the children of working people; it should remain "Peon U." But Zook persisted, and a $3,000,000 bond issue to facilitate the move was placed on the November 1929 ballot. On October 24, however, the New York Stock Exchange experienced the first traumatic shock of what was to become the Great Depression, and two weeks later voters rejected every money issue on the ballot. Relocation was dead, but another four years of wishful thinking prevented the Board from taking any action to improve campus facilities. Disheartened, Zook left for a position as U.S. Commissioner of Higher Education, where he exerted admirable leadership.

The Akron campus inherited by President Hezzleton E. Simmons in 1933 was essentially the same that he had known as a Buchtel College student. Space was so limited that the University had to raise admission standards as a means of controlling enrollment. By the 1930s these standards were among the highest in Ohio, yet worthy students were crowded out. Simmons finally was able to persuade his conservative Board to apply for funds from two federal work-relief agencies, the Works Progress Administration and the Public Works Administration. Money from the former was used to build Simmons Hall (so named at the request of enthusiastic students) and money from the latter to build the student center, which was later absorbed into an expanded Gardner Student Center.

Simmons also had to contend with the "G.I. Bulge." Starting in 1945, demobilized World War II veterans flocked to colleges all over America, including Akron's tiny campus. Every conceivable space on or near the campus was converted to classroom use, and ugly but functional "temporary" buildings were erected on the central campus. Some relief came when Akron voters approved building levies that led to the construction of Ayer Hall (on the site of Phillips Hall, formerly the president's house) and of Knight Hall (later refurbished and renamed Crouse Hall). Convinced that Akron voters would not stand for "frills," the Board of Directors insisted on plain, rectangular structures. The architectural style could be described as "factory modern," but offered maximum square footage for the dollar.

Simmons did well under extremely trying conditions, but much remained to be accomplished when Norman P. Auburn assumed the presidency in 1951. Auburn recognized that voters seldom understand all that goes on within a university's walls. Most, he felt, rate an institution's worth according to what they can see—its physical plant. Campus growth and beautification, therefore, were good public relations.

Voter support was vital to the University. Auburn set out immediately to organize campaigns to raise money through municipal tax levies. The entire campus was mobilized. Faculty, staff, and students canvassed neighborhoods, and on voting day they handed out literature to voters approaching the polling places. Every city precinct was covered. The most dramatic campaign (one whose aim was to obtain operating as opposed to building funds) was the 1958 effort to amend the city charter for the benefit of the University. Out of 95,626 votes cast by Akron citizens, the issue was defeated by 64 votes. The Board of Directors authorized a recount. An astonishing number of ballots had been marked incorrectly, and the recount gave the University a 262-vote victory.

Although building levies were essential, public money had to be supplemented with private funds to achieve urgently needed improvements. Here, too, Auburn moved vigorously. Private monies from fund-raising campaigns helped to construct Memorial Hall and Parke R. Kolbe Hall in the early 1950s. In that same period a Firestone family gift made it possible to purchase the St. Paul's Episcopal

Church buildings at Market and Forge Streets. A combination of public and private funds enabled the University to acquire what was described as the nation's first university-sponsored urban renewal district: 23 acres south of Carroll Street. Scores of houses and a few small businesses were razed, and Lee R. Jackson Field was developed on the land. This large addition had a dramatic impact, opening up the campus and providing room for athletics, recreation, and relaxation.

Every move to expand the campus necessarily required families or businesses to relocate. Most transactions were handled smoothly and equitably, a matter of prime importance if voter backlash was to be avoided, but occasionally people opposed the acquisition of a particular property. One such case involved Terry's Place on Buchtel Avenue across from the campus, a dingy, wooden saloon that stank of stale beer. A number of students and faculty lamented its passing, and angry letters-to-the-editor accused the University of hounding an honest businessman out of his property just to build parking lots. But their efforts went for naught. Thirsty students could still find refreshment at nearby Schroeder's on Center Street until it too fell to campus expansion.

Barriers that once limited campus growth were broken in every direction during Auburn's twenty-year presidency. The University District, in which no incompatible building was to be allowed, kept expanding until it embraced almost the entire area bounded on the west by the railroad tracks, on the north by Market Street, on the east by the Akron Expressway, and on the south by Exchange Street. Within this district, campus development followed a typical pattern. The University would acquire a building, adapt it for use, tear it down for parking, and later erect a new building on the site. In some cases—Spicer School, the Akron Union Depot, the Haven of Rest, and the Akron Bible Institute, for instance—a solid building was converted to more permanent use.

A bold thrust that combined physical expansion with a new university policy was Auburn's move to build dormitories. By diversifying the student population he hoped to broaden the contacts of the essentially local student body. Having resident students would also encourage a more collegiate atmosphere. And so, for the first time since Buchtel College days, the campus had dormitory students; they were accommodated in a number of buildings erected north of Buchtel Avenue.

The University District was further improved by the razing of ugly business buildings across Sumner Street to make way for the modern Norman Paul Auburn Science and Engineering Center. The former Buchtel Academy building, then known as Olin Hall, was demolished to make way for a broad pedestrian walkway that bridged Sumner Street. Another bridge extended south across Carroll Street to Harry P. Schrank Hall. Schrank Hall was noteworthy for external design flourishes that broke the mold of bland utilitarianism characteristic of most University buildings.

While the campus was reaching out in every direction, changes went on apace in the central area. The student center was expanded several times. In the process old Crouse Gym was razed, as was a nondescript little building once used as an ROTC armory. Carl Kolbe Hall, housing Bierce Library, gave way to a new library building, which in turn would lose its collections to a new Bierce

Library. The former library building endures as Carroll
Hall. Leigh Hall was built on the site of the original Knight
Chemical Laboratory, and Zook Hall occupied a corner of
the land on which Old Buchtel once stood. During exca-
vations for Zook and its connecting utilities tunnel, rem-
nants of dishes and kitchenware dating back to the 1899
fire were recovered.

Fire struck the central campus again in 1971 when Buchtel Hall was gutted by a blaze. Sentiment was divided on
the issue of how best to rebuild, but those who wanted to
save Buchtel Hall prevailed and it was converted into administrative offices. Today each office suite carries the
name of a Buchtel College president.

Prior to his retirement in 1971, Auburn organized the
plans and financing for a striking new structure, the Ed-
win J. Thomas Performing Arts Hall. This magnificent
building stood on ground once occupied by John R. Buch-

tel's Buckeye Mower and Reaper Company. A private fund-raising venture, said to be the largest to date by a public university in Ohio, provided the bulk of the funds. The building was completed during the presidency of Dominic J. Guzzetta and was dedicated in 1973.

Guzzetta maintained the building pace as University enrollments soared. The new Olin Hall was completed; the City of Akron transferred the Rubber Bowl to the University; a new home for the College of Fine and Applied Arts was named for Dominic and Nola Guzzetta; the new Knight Chemical Laboratory, the college of nursing's Mary Gladwin Hall, the computer center, and the C. Blake McDowell Law Center helped fill out the campus's west end, as did the refurbishing of the Akron Union Depot into the Buckingham Center for Continuing Education. Exchange Street was crossed; the University acquired the East Crown apartment complex for dormitories, and a former Holiday Inn became Gallucci Hall. In that same area a former Cadillac agency was converted into splendid quarters for the school of art.

A long-awaited campus addition completed during this period was the James A. Rhodes Health and Physical Education Building, built on the site of a city fire station that was relocated to make room for it. In conjunction with the nearby Ocasek Natatorium, the Rhodes Arena provided the campus with modern athletic facilities.

Soon after William V. Muse assumed the presidency in 1984, two long-standing dreams became reality. First the University campus "spanned the tracks." For decades both city and University officials had talked of uniting the campus with Akron's main downtown district. One plan had been to connect Thomas Hall's plaza with the city's

Morley Health Center on Broadway. In the late 1980s, however, the University acquired the former Polsky's department store on Main Street, along with its large parking deck. The former Greyhound bus terminal on Broadway was also acquired as the site for a new college of business administration building.

The second major development was Buchtel Common. Akron city officials were persuaded to vacate Buchtel Avenue and reroute its traffic to a new road that bypassed the center of campus. Street paving was removed and replaced by a red-brick, landscaped pathway that extended throughout the central campus area. Among the new amenities gracing the Common were a statue of John R. Buchtel as part of the redesigned approach to Buchtel Hall, and the Dorothy Garrett Martin Fountain, located at the main junction of campus walkways.

President Muse promoted the use of Hower House for social functions and other events. Donated to the University in the 1970s by the descendants of Akron industrialist John Hower, this grand Second Empire house on Fir Hill is a tangible link with the world of John R. Buchtel and his associates. The University also remodeled the recently acquired University Club, and the Graduate School occupied a refurbished mansion nearby.

Most striking of all is the "polymer tower," which houses the College of Polymer Science and Polymer Engineering. This twelve-story structure, with its unusual shape and reflecting facade, promises to become an architectural landmark by which the University will be identified in the future.

This brief journey through the Akron campus can only suggest the hard work, the imagination, and the faith that went into its creation. Hundreds of talented people had a hand in planning, financing, constructing, and maintaining the emerging campus and its buildings. Only one who can visualize the tiny campus as it once was can fully appreciate the magnitude of the change. Where else in America has a university absorbed for its own use the city's major railroad depot, a large department store, a bus terminal, a major city street, a public school, a municipal stadium, several churches, a Bible institute, a rehabilitation center, two automobile agencies, a Holiday Inn, a postal substation, a major apartment complex, and any number of business and residential properties? Yet the pressure for further expansion remains as enrollments continue at a high level and faculty research increases in volume and sophistication.

What would the Ohio Universalists of a hundred years ago think of their college now? Undoubtedly most would approve. As for John R. Buchtel, enterprising, large-minded, public-spirited, we can only believe that he would be "as happy as a clam in high water."

17

Change and Continuity

 healthy society learns from the past: it does not live in the past. This glimpse into the University's history reveals the pervasiveness of change. In nearly every visible way The University of Akron appears to differ totally from old Buchtel College, but this perception captures only a portion of reality. The goal of the University—to produce educated men and women—is as clear as it ever was, even if our concept of what constitutes an educated person has changed. The central activity—learning—is no different, though it takes different forms. It may be appropriate to summarize present conditions that represent a definite break with the past, and then to seek out the continuities that unite the present with the past. First, the changes.

Buchtel College, like most institutions of its time, was church-related. In a society that believed in or at least gave lip service to the centrality of spiritual life, it was appropriate for religious denominations to give their young people an educational experience consistent with denominational beliefs. Buchtel had no religious tests, however, and welcomed all comers who were prepared to profit from the work it had to offer. The church connection lapsed formally in 1907, even before the College's transformation to public status made it inappropriate. In the public University, clergymen no longer served as president and chapel services disappeared. The puritanical behavior advocated by nearly all Protestant religious bodies in that age slowly gave way to more latitudinarian practices.

Before specialized and practical courses undermined it, the old classical curriculum emphasized learning for its own sake. In nineteenth-century society an educated person could use his or her talents in an unlimited number of occupations. Buchtel graduates with classical training were active in every profession, in business and commerce, in politics, farming, invention, and entrepreneurship. As society's needs changed, collegiate curricula accommodated them with an array of specialized courses, although a rearguard action managed to preserve a vestige of the traditional. Today's students expect their college experiences to prepare them to fill a specific employment niche. Whatever intellectual broadening the student receives from general studies requirements or from electives is seen as a bonus. Humanities majors still resemble the traditionally trained college student of yore; they tend to lack clear job goals and are anxious about finding a position that will not require them to "sell out" their interests for a salary.

Buchtel College, of course, was a teaching college. Edward Claypole, Charles Knight, and others who pursued their interests through research as well as teaching were highly respected, but there was no ambivalence about what constituted the faculty member's principal duty—it was classroom instruction. Today's university properly emphasizes both instruction and research. Graduate degrees are research-oriented, and the great growth of such offerings necessitates a faculty capable of providing a professional model for the student.

The relationship of the student to the institution is more than merely one of learner to instructor. A good deal of a student's life is lived within academic confines, and in earlier times colleges imposed severe restrictions on student manners and mores. Buchtel, like all colleges of its time, practiced the principle of *in loco parentis,* serving in place of parents to assure a moral and ethical environment for its charges. Not only was everyone known to everyone else, but social conformity was mandated and practiced. For many decades after 1913, The University of Akron, though a public institution, retained that extended-family ambience, and university officials were as ready to impose their behavioral expectations on students as their predecessors had been. Students of the 1920s, 1930s, and 1940s well remember that Dean Elizabeth Thompson, Dean Donfred Gardner, and their associates ran a tight ship. Today's students, operating in a much more open environment, cannot imagine how threatening it was to be called to account by these watchdogs of campus propriety.

Society has changed radically in the past few decades. Eighteen-year-olds are legal adults and as such cannot be deprived of certain rights. Grades can no longer be posted or placed where others, including parents, can see them. Due process procedures for students accused of wrongdoing are elaborate and cumbersome. The "pill" and women's liberation have overturned traditional constraints on female students. Blacks and other minorities assert their rights. It is truly a different social world.

Other manifestations of change are also apparent, if not

so pervasive and important. Intercollegiate athletics have evolved from strictly amateur club sports to well-subsidized, popularly marketed events. The public did not think less of Buchtel College when it lost to its competitors; but today so much of an institution's reputation in the community and in the nation depends on the records of its athletic teams that tremendous attention is paid to won-and-lost records. Other student activities have become professionalized beyond anything known to Buchtel College or to the Municipal University. Music, art, communications, theater, publications, and many other areas operate on a level that no one would have imagined a half-century or more ago.

Change is so evident that it sometimes conceals continuity, but continuity in fact dominates. Students are still students. At their best they are eager, optimistic, anxious, and ready to prepare for an important social role. They come, however, in every description. The expansion of housing in recent decades has opened the campus to students from many parts of the state, nation, and world. They join a strong local contingent, including great numbers of older, so-called "nontraditional" students, a clientele that the University has always served in both day and evening classes. In essence, students are what they have always been.

What is true of students is also true of faculty. Many of the same motivations that have always lured persons to the classroom continue to do so. A way of life, a love affair with a discipline, a missionary zeal to impart knowledge, a sense of independence, a liking for students, the desire to discover new knowledge, all continue to direct men and women to faculty positions.

Faculty members disagree, as they have for the past century, on how best to package four years of course work into a baccalaureate degree. The contest will never end; it will evolve as new knowledge, social pressures, technology, and other forces come into play, but it will endure. The debate often centers on the General Studies program, which provides a strong thread of continuity that leads back to the classical curriculum of Buchtel College. That program is best seen as an effort, however modest, to assure that all students are forced to move beyond their narrow interests into contact with the intellectual, artistic, and societal concerns that have occupied mankind for millennia. The particular makeup of these required courses is not sacrosanct; changes are always in the wind. What is sacrosanct is the notion of broadening one's horizons.

Service to students is another force for continuity. Rarely has Buchtel College or The University of Akron failed to put the student's well-being first. It might not always appear so to a student who is seeking special consideration or has run afoul of a rule that appears too restrictive. But the records of the student personnel office and campus folklore are replete with examples of faculty members and administrators going to great lengths to serve student needs. A classroom is not a democracy, yet most instructors adhere to democratic principles when seeking to help their students. On a more formal level, offices of student counseling, testing, employment, health, and financial aid demonstrate the University's sincerity in meeting student needs. And on the extracurricular or co-curricular side, the University, as it always has, encourages and supports student organizations that offer experiences likely to be useful to young men and women after they have left the special world of the campus.

One final evidence of continuity will have to suffice. Since the first class convened in Old Buchtel in September 1872, quality and excellence have been emphasized as the lodestones of the educational process on the Hilltop campus. Like Western Reserve and many other midwestern colleges, Buchtel had a standard of excellence—Yale—to which it aspired and on which it modeled itself. The College celebrated excellence in its faculty by bestowing its limited rewards on Kolbe, Knight, Claypole, Olin, and other luminaries. It rewarded its students' accomplishments by founding honor societies to recognize them.

The Municipal University also sought excellence. Its model was Cincinnati, commonly regarded as the epitome of what a municipal university should be. Akron in turn became the model for the municipal institution that is now Detroit's Wayne State University and for Topeka's Washburn University. Like Buchtel, the Municipal University was quick to honor student accomplishment and to recognize faculty excellence. Since there were but few publishing faculty members in those days, reputations were largely local; but what student fortunate enough to sit at their feet could forget Samuel Selby, Fred Griffin, Hjalmar Distad, Arthur Young, Don Keister, Charles Duffy, Helen and Robert Thackaberry, Walter Kraatz, Summerfield Baldwin, Frank Simonetti, Ray Pease, Emily Davis, Kenneth Cochrane, Tom Evans, Andy Maluke, Donfred Gardner, and Warren and Julia Leigh? One measure of their skill was the success their students enjoyed in the nation's great graduate and professional schools.

Today's University continues to aspire to the best. With a high percentage of honors students, with faculty in virtually every department offering invigorating classroom instruction, with admirable researchers directing student apprentices, with ever-better facilities and support services, it moves with the fast-changing world while holding fast to the truths that have served it so well for the past 120 years.

University Buildings and Properties

On the rapidly changing Akron campus, any listing of building names can be up-to-date only for the moment. This list identifies buildings and other facilities which, with few exceptions, were named for people.

NORMAN PAUL AUBURN SCIENCE AND ENGINEERING CENTER (1968)

Honors Auburn, architect of state status and president of the University (1951–71).

AYER HALL (1949)

Named for Frederic E. Ayer, first dean of the College of Engineering (1914–46).

BIERCE LIBRARY (1973)

Named for Gen. Lucius V. Bierce, Akron attorney and community leader, whose contribution of books and funds established the Buchtel College Library.

Muehlstein Rare Book Room. Honors the donor of rare books, Herman Muehlstein, a prominent New York businessman.

John S. Knight Reading Room. Pulitzer Prize–winning editor of the *Akron Beacon Journal.* His papers are in the University Archives, where this room is located.

BUCHTEL COMMON (1989)

This landscaped walkway occupies what was once Buchtel Avenue.

Dorothy Garrett Martin Fountain. Donated in 1989 by Paul E. Martin, Class of '35, in honor of his wife Dorothy, Class of '38, on the occasion of their 50th wedding anniversary.

BUCHTEL FIELD (1892)

No record shows its official name, but it has always been known as Buchtel Field. It was the site of Alumni Memorial Stadium, erected in 1923 to honor Summit County's World War I dead.

BUCHTEL HALL (1901)

Named for John R. Buchtel, a founder of Buchtel College, this building partially replaced Old Buchtel, the original college building destroyed by fire in 1899.

McCollester Suite. Honors Sullivan McCollester, president of Buchtel College 1872–78.

Rexford Suite. Honors Everett L. Rexford, president of Buchtel College 1878–80.

Cone Suite. Named for Orello Cone, president of Buchtel College 1880–96.

Knight Suite. Charles M. Knight, a longtime professor, was president of Buchtel College 1896–97.

Priest Suite. Named for Ira Priest, president of Buchtel College 1897–1902.

Church Suite. Named for Augustus B. Church, president of Buchtel College 1902–12.

Greeley Lobby. Horace Greeley, editor of the *New York Tribune* and 1872 presidential candidate, delivered the address at the cornerstone-laying ceremony for the original Buchtel Hall, July 4, 1871.

BUCKINGHAM CENTER FOR CONTINUING EDUCATION (1979)

The Buckingham Center is the former Akron Union Depot. Remodeled in 1979, it is named for local attorney, philanthropist, and university trustee Lisle Buckingham.

CARROLL HALL (1949 and 1961)

Built in two stages to house the Bierce Library collection, it was converted to other uses. It is identified with its location on Carroll Street, which was named for a nineteenth-century Akron real estate developer.

CROUSE HALL (1951)

Originally called Knight Hall, this building was renamed for Akron business leader George W. Crouse, trustee and benefactor of Buchtel College.

EAST HALL (1972)

Formerly the United Brethren Church, purchased by the University to house a variety of programs.

FOLK HALL (1984)

Converted from an automobile agency to house the School of Art, this building is named for Akron businessman Harold K. Folk and his wife Catherine F. Folk.

Emily Davis Gallery. Honors Emily Davis, professor of art and former head of the Department of Art.

GARDNER STUDENT CENTER (1939)

Much modified and expanded since it was built in 1939, this building is named for Donfred H. Gardner, dean of students and later vice president and dean of administration.

Perkins Gallery. Honors a distinguished early Akron family.

MARY GLADWIN HALL (1979)

Mary Gladwin, Class of 1887, had a distinguished international nursing career and was influential in the American Red Cross.

GUZZETTA HALL (1976)

Honors Dominic J. Guzzetta, president of the University 1971–84, and his wife, Nola M. Guzzetta.

Firestone Conservatory. The School of Music facilities honor Akron's Firestone family.

Sandefur Experimental Theater. Honors Ray M. Sandefur, first dean of the College of Fine and Applied Arts.

Nola Guzzetta Recital Hall. Honors Nola M. Guzzetta, wife of president Dominic J. Guzzetta.

HEISMAN LODGE (1988)

Located at the Rubber Bowl, it is named for John W. Heisman, Buchtel College coach in 1893–94.

HOWER HOUSE (1973)

This Fir Hill mansion, now on the National Register of Historic Buildings, was built by Akron industrialist John Hower in 1871, and was donated to the University by his descendants.

JACKSON FIELD (1964)

Named for Lee Jackson, ex '11 Buchtel College athlete, Akron business leader, and chairman of the board of the University.

Knight Chemical Laboratory (1979)

This is the third building to bear the name of Charles M. Knight, professor of chemistry, founder of collegiate instruction in rubber chemistry, and president of Buchtel College 1896–97.

Kolbe Hall (1955)

Honors Parke R. Kolbe, Class of '01, president of Buchtel College 1912–13, architect of municipal status, and first president of The Municipal University of Akron (1913–25).

Leigh Hall (1965)

Named for Warren W. Leigh, first dean of the College of Business Administration.

Knight Auditorium. Honors John S. Knight, former publisher and editor of the *Akron Beacon Journal*.

C. Blake McDowell Law Center (1973)

Named for an Akron attorney and philanthropist.

Judge W. E. Pardee Court Room. Honors William E. Pardee, distinguished jurist appointed to the original 9th District Court of Appeals of Ohio.

Albrecht Memorial Room. Gift of Albrecht Inc. and the Fred W. Albrecht Grocery Company.

Memorial Hall (1954)

Honors Summit County's World War II dead.

Cochrane Gym. Dedicated in 1989 in honor of Kenneth "Red" Cochrane, Class of '32, athlete, coach, professor of physical education, and athletic director.

Maluke Pool. Dedicated in 1989 in honor of Andrew W. "Andy" Maluke, Class of '44, who spent forty-five years on campus as student, coach, professor of physical education, and head of the department of physical education.

Ocasek Natatorium (1988)

Honors former professor of education and state senator Oliver R. Ocasek.

Cliff Skeen Weight Room. Named for Ohio representative Cliff Skeen.

Olin Hall (1976)

The second building to carry this name, Olin Hall honors Charles R. Olin and Oscar E. Olin. Charles, Class of '85, was a Buchtel College administrator. Oscar was a highly regarded professor and administrator.

Theodore T. Duke Memorial Auditorium. Honors a member of the Class of '39, a distinguished professor of classics and former head of the Department of Classics.

Clara G. Roe Seminar Room. Honors a professor of history and former head of the Department of History.

Emile Grunberg Reading Room. Honors a professor of economics and former head of the Department of Economics.

Thackaberry Library. In honor of Helen and Robert Thackaberry, faculty members who offered distinguished service to the Department of English.

Laurence Lafleur Memorial Library. Honors a professor of philosophy and former head of the Department of Philosophy.

Olson Research Center (1983)

The former Olson Electronics Warehouse was redesigned and named for benefactors Sidney L. Olson and his wife Miriam.

Residence Halls

Sisler-McFawn. Named for the Akron foundation that contributed to its construction.

Orr. Named for Gertrude Orr, mother of Owen Orr, a local businessman whose contributions made the building possible.

Ritchie. Named for the Akron foundation that contributed to its construction.

Bulger. Charles Bulger, Class of '08, a longtime faculty member, was dean of the Buchtel College of Liberal Arts and later dean of graduate studies.

Garson. Named for local businessman Richard S. Garson.

Spanton. Albert I. Spanton, Class of '99, was a longtime faculty member and dean of the Buchtel College of Liberal Arts.

Gallucci. Named for local businessman Michael Gallucci, whose generosity enabled the University to acquire this property.

Robertson Dining Hall. Named in honor of Helen, Class of '20, and James G. Robertson, local philanthropists.

James A. Rhodes Health and Physical Education Building (1985)

Named for former governor James A. Rhodes, who encouraged appropriations in support of many campus buildings.

Evans Lounge. Honors Tommy Evans, respected coach and former professor of physical education.

Rubber Bowl (1940)

This 35,000-seat stadium, located four miles from campus, was transferred by the City of Akron to the University. It is used for football and special events.

Schrank Hall (1969)

Named in honor of Harry P. Schrank, Class of '24, local businessman and longtime chairman of the University's board of trustees.

Petry Auditorium. Named in memory of William M. Petry, first dean of the Community and Technical College.

Simmons Hall (1936)

Honors Hezzleton E. Simmons, Class of '08, professor of chemistry and president of the University 1933–51.

Spicer Hall (1975)

This former Akron public school building was renovated in 1975 to house University administrative offices. It was named for members of Akron's pioneer family.

Edwin J. Thomas Performing Arts Hall (1973)

Thomas Hall honors the former chairman of the Goodyear Tire and Rubber Company and a University trustee.

James G. Robertson Lobby. Honors an Akron business leader.

Benjamin Franklin Goodrich Lobby. Honors the founder of Akron's rubber industry.

E. C. McCormick, Jr. Lobby. Honors a prominent local businessman, Class of '23, and his wife Alberta, Class of '25.

Thomas Tower. Honors John W. Thomas, Class of '04, Akron business leader and former chairman of the board of directors.

Charles Herberich Lobby. Honors an Akron businessman.

Shea Tower. In memory of Mrs. John Shea.

Dr. Louis A. Witzeman Counterweights. Honors a distinguished Akron physician.

Lee Jackson Balcony. Honors a prominent Akron businessman, ex '11.

Joseph Mayl Memorial Balcony. In memory of a local businessman.

Lois Bishop DeYoung Balcony Bridge. Honors a prominent Akronite, ex '33.

C. C. Dilley Balcony Bridge. Honors a local businessman.

Pardee Lobby. Named in honor of Judge and Mrs. William E. Pardee.

C. Blake McDowell Office Wing. Honors an Akron attorney and philanthropist.

Clara I. Knight Plaza. Named for the mother of John S. Knight, former publisher and editor of the *Akron Beacon Journal.*

UNIVERSITY CLUB (1978)

Originally a private club, this facility was acquired by the University Foundation for community and university functions.

WEST HALL (1971)

Formerly the Akron Bible Institute, this building was acquired for classroom and office use.

WHITBY HALL (1973)

Named for George Stafford Whitby, premier rubber chemist and a founder of the present Institute for Polymer Research.

ZOOK HALL (1963)

Named in honor of George F. Zook, president of the University 1925–33.

Index

This book was composed in Palatino, a contemporary typeface
by Hermann Zapf.
It was typeset by Brevis Press, Bethany Connecticut,
on a Mergenthaler 202.
It was printed by R. R. Donnelley & Sons Co., Harrisonburg, Virginia.
It was designed and produced by Kachergis Book Design,
Pittsboro, North Carolina.